In Search of Sleep

In Search of
Sleep

STRAIGHT TALK ABOUT BABIES, TODDLERS AND NIGHT WAKING

Bonny Reichert

TODAY'S PARENT

SARASOTA PRESS

U.S. Cataloging-in-Publication Data is available upon request

Canadian Cataloging-in-Publication Data
Reichert, Bonny
    In search of sleep : straight talk about babies, toddlers and night waking

ISBN 1-55356-008-6

1. Infants – Sleep.   2. Toddlers – Sleep.   3. Sleep disorders in childern – Popular works.
I. Title.

RJ506.S55R44 2001   649'.122   C00-933228-6

The publisher gratefully acknowledges the support of the Canada Council for the Arts and the Ontario Arts Council for its publishing program.

We acknowledge the financial support of the Government of Canada through the Book Publishing Industry Development Program (BPIDP) for our publishing activities.

Sarasota Press
is an imprint of Key Porter Books Limited
4808 South Tamiami Trail
PMB #205
Sarasota, Florida
34231-4352

Key Porter Books Limited
70 The Esplanade
Toronto, Ontario
Canada M5E 1R4

www.keyporter.com

Design: Peter Maher
Photography: Kathleen Finlay
Electronic formatting: Jean Lightfoot Peters

PUBLISHER'S NOTE: This publication provides general information about children and sleep. It does not contain medical advice. While the parties believe that the contents of this publication are accurate, a licensed medical practitioner should be consulted in the event that medical advice is desired.

Printed and bound in Canada

01 02 03 04 05 6 5 4 3 2

Acknowledgments

It's not just that many different people help you write a book like the one you are holding, but that they provide so many different kinds of help.

James McKenna's remarkable sleep research and his patience in answering my questions have been indispensable.

Meredith F. Small's fascinating book, *Our Babies, Ourselves*, offered valuable background information and inspiration, especially for Chapter Seven, "Half a World Away."

Big thanks go to Holly Bennett of Today's Parent for being the most gentle, intelligent editor a writer could hope for, and to John Hoffman for his keen insights, like the one that sparked his term "expert tunnel vision" (which I borrowed in Chapter Four). Thanks also to Linda Pruessen, Clare McKeon and Key Porter Books for their flexibility and expertise.

I am indebted to the hundreds of parents—a few of them friends but most strangers—who bravely shared the details of their night lives with me in the spirit of helping other moms, dads and kids. Also to my own parents, as well as my sisters and in-laws, who helped in various, sundry and sometimes unexpected ways.

Finally I need to thank my children, James and Leo, who sparkle even in the darkest part of the night, and without whom there would be no book. And my husband, Michael, who completes me and just about everything I do.

Contents

Preface
CONFESSIONS OF A FAILED SLEEP TRAINER

When I first told a friend that I had been approached to write a book on kids' night waking, she looked at me incredulously and snorted, *"You're* going to write a book on babies and sleep? You're just such an expert, huh?"* At that point, my 9-month-old was waking two to six times each night.

My girlfriend was absolutely right. I am definitely not an expert on getting kids to sleep through the night. But as the mother of an 8-year-old who didn't snooze a solid ten hours until he was 4 (someone once thought I meant months—that's *years*) and a 14-month-old who has no interest in breaking with family tradition, I do know a little something about night waking. And after spending five years as an editor at *Today's Parent* magazine, I've also learned a thing or two about listening to moms and dads.

As it turns out, this background—more than hours logged at a sleep clinic—has been essential. In putting together *In Search of Sleep*, I've corresponded with over 200 parents. As I've read or listened to a colorful assortment of opinions and a range of nighttime practices, the ideas central to this book have taken shape and evolved.

As you flip pages, you're going to find passages that are frankly critical of sleep-training techniques such as "controlled crying" or "extinction," and the experts who have devised them. Most of this criticism is based on feedback collected from parents who found that sleep training didn't work for their families, either practically or philosophically. But that does not mean that sleep training fails every parent. Nor does it mean—and I want to shout this from the rooftops—that there is anything wrong with parents choosing to sleep train their kids. Guilt is such a big occupational hazard of parenting. Please don't let this book contribute to yours. Your own instincts and family circumstances matter more than any sleep book, this one included.

The truth is, I started out wanting to sleep train my kids. When my feisty first-born didn't sleep through the night at 3 or 6 or 9 months, I took a friend's advice and ran to the store to pick up a book temptingly titled *Solve Your Child's Sleep Problems*.

Something about the method didn't feel quite right from the get-go, but neither did getting up every two hours, so we persevered. At the end of the first week, Jamie was still waking up three times a night and crying with gusto. What were we doing wrong? Desperately, I reread my books. I interrogated parents with sleeping babes. If they said they sang Simon and Garfunkel before lights out, I belted out "Feeling Groovy." If their tots went down at 7:48, Jamie hit the sack at the same time. But nothing seemed to work consistently, or for very long. We'd get a few restful nights and then he'd catch a cold or cut a tooth and we'd say, No, we just can't do it tonight. Eventually, we gave up completely and allowed our sleeping arrangements to become a jumble of rocking, nursing, tiptoeing and musical beds.

Fast-forward a handful of years. Jamie grows into James, a confident kid who happily slumbers solo each night. At 7, he becomes a big brother and I find myself back in babyland, this time, not so young and inexperienced. Still, I become insecure when I begin getting flak about little Leo's night waking. "Maybe we shouldn't run to him when he cries at night," I say to my husband. It's as if some kind of amnesia strikes. "He's just a tiny baby," I say. "How long can he cry? How bad can it be?"

The intervening years spent reading about parenthood, talking to other moms and dads—working at a parenting magazine, for God's sake!—don't make the slightest difference. Forty minutes into our first attempt to sleep train Leo, we're wringing our hands and pulling at our hair. Enough. As we climb the stairs to Leo's room, we tell each other that we do not *have* to sleep train our baby. Who cares what the neighbors say? That evening, and many evenings since then, we agree that going to a baby three times a night, or driving around until he's asleep, or bringing him into bed with us is not a mistake. It's a choice.

If your kids were born sleeping through the night, then these are choices you've never had to make. If not, keep reading.

1 You Are Not Alone

INTRODUCING THE NIGHT-WAKING COMMUNITY

One steamy morning last summer, I was parking our stroller among several others as my 1-year-old and I arrived at our weekly playgroup. We were a few weeks into the session, so I knew the other babies and parents just well enough to smile and say hello. I'm not sure what made me go a step further and, addressing no one in particular, say, "Wow, I feel great. Leo slept through till 5 a.m. this morning for the first time." Six or seven heads snapped up from unbuckling seat belts to look at me. I felt as though I had just revealed that I was wearing leather underwear. "But he hasn't been waking up all this time, has he?" one mom said, not unkindly. "Yes he has," I said. There was silence as the others digested this information, and, I guess, the fact that I was sharing it. Then the stories started bubbling up. "Well, you know, my daughter doesn't really sleep through the night either." "Mine does, as long as one of us gets up to give her her pacifier a few times a night." "Well at least it's just a pacifier, our son wants to be rocked back to sleep each time he wakes up . . . ."

Who are the parents dealing with night waking? You might assume they'd be the most rumpled in every crowd, out there doing desperate things: sleeping in their clothes in order to get just a few extra minutes of shut-eye in the morning, or napping on park benches while their kids gobble handfuls of playground sand and God-knows-what-else.

Of course the real picture is not nearly so bleak. Perhaps there are tired parents who lock their keys in the car once in a while (guilty!) or get nothing but pizza or Kraft Dinner on the table for 6 p.m. But they also chat animatedly about their child's first words at the office water cooler and peacefully push the swing beside you at the park. They act normal. They look together. Most of the time, they cope better than expected. I bet you do, too.

What they might not be doing is talking about their kids' night waking. Many parents would sooner show you their birth video or divulge their marital problems than tell you their 1½-year-old needs to be rocked back to sleep a couple of times a night. We tend to keep a lid on our kids' sleep quirks.

After all, telling the truth is risky business. Just ask Laura Galloway. "My baby, who is now 19 months old, never was a great sleeper. I've adopted the same sleeping habits as her (minus the naps, of course!). I'm quite happy with the arrangement. However, I know that I am being judged and criticized by many friends and (especially!) family members, who think my child is setting the rules in our house with regard to bed-time. So, for the most part, I don't bring up the subject, for I don't want to feel I have to defend my parenting style."

Galloway is one of nearly 1,500 parents who responded to the *Today's Parent* Sleep Survey, conducted through the magazine and *Today's Parent* Online in the summer of 1999. Moms and dads from Moose Jaw, Saskatchewan, to Goose Neck, South Carolina, revealed in writing what they often have trouble saying out loud.

Tirsa Thompson, mom to 10-month-old Zacchari, puts it this way: "Our son sleeps with us, which we have decided is the best way for us to maintain that close contact with him. Not only that, we all seem to get a better night's sleep. Through conversations I have had with others with young children, we have found that most other parents' babies and children do not sleep through the night in their own beds, either. Furthermore, we all handle the situation in the same manner: LIE. 'Oh yes, he is sleeping through the night.' We have all found this avoids fur-ther comments or criticisms."

What happens when people like Thompson feel they must cover up the truth about their babies' sleep habits—and their own? They avoid confrontation, yes, but meanwhile, the big myth—that sleeping through the night is the norm for babies from an impossibly tender age—is per-petuated. In addition, meaningful communication between parents is sabotaged; instead of supporting each other through one of the most challenging aspects of parenthood, we end up feeling that we have to defend our choice, or hide it.

Then, when someone like Shelley Yaremcio finds herself in the thick of night waking with no support network, the struggle intensifies. Shelley doesn't know Tirsa or anyone like her, so she feels isolated as well as exhausted. "My baby, Cory, is 9 months old and cried as an infant whenever I was not holding him. I am just starting to try and put him down in his crib for naps as he only sleeps while driving or while being pushed in his stroller. I know my friends are tired of hearing it and I get the impression that they feel I am just a bad mom, but I have tried everything and he just wants to be with me. I have even lost friendships as no one understands how exhausted I constantly am. I wish they could step in my shoes so they could understand. I guess they really aren't true friends but it hurts nonetheless."

It's a shame that night waking is so often layered with feelings of loneliness and even guilt, because the moms and dads of sleepless kids already have a pretty tough time. Yes, all parents have days when our hearts are so full of pride and happiness and love that we think they'll burst right through our chests. But there are also the nights. Waking to find a wee hour glowing on the bedside clock, a sleepless child and dark silence on all sides can be rather unnerving. How much worse if you are certain that everybody else in your time zone is blissfully unplugged: babies tucked sweetly into their cribs, moms and dads racking up a solid seven hours. Most of what you read or hear about kids and sleep—that night waking will lead to greater problems later on, that it's just not normal—will probably add to your feeling that you are all alone.

Into the Light

But you're not. Read on and you'll discover that you are part of a community of people around the world who tend to their children once, twice, three or more times a night. Some of these parents do so willingly; others are not so keen. You'll hear from a few who actually like nighttime duty, as well one or two who are so worn out they're truly desperate. Most fall in between. The night-waking community this book draws from is spread throughout Canada and the U.S.; it reaches as far as Europe and Australia. It is made up of mothers and fathers who came to parenting earlier or later in life, with diverse cultural backgrounds. Their attitudes range from "We have a family bed and are proud of it" to "I was a wife before I was a mother and the marital bed is just for my husband and me"; from "I wanna be there every second" to "I just can't cope." Some are surprised to find themselves on the "wrong" side of a debate that rages, however quietly, through the ranks of parents and experts, or to find themselves adopting solutions they once thought unacceptable.

You won't agree with all of these parents. However, after reading their stories, you'll discover that you're one of them. That alone won't help your baby sleep through the night and it won't make you feel more rested, but it *will* help you shake the feeling that there is something fundamentally wrong with a baby who wakes at night, or with parents who do their very best to care for that baby. With a little luck, you may even start to feel good about your child's night waking, and the approach you take to it.

This book is a response to the societal pressures faced by parents of night wakers. I hope it will help you unload your night-waking baggage, because in our society, night waking is about a lot more than lost sleep. As I delved into standard sleep lore and compared it to night lives across North America, I became increasingly aware that our discomfort with less-than-textbook children's sleep habits is not just practical, but societal, emotional and even moral. I also learned that these attitudes tend to make night waking and some of its antidotes (like bed sharing) taboo subjects. They inhibit straight talk about kids and sleep, so that we end up dismissing as idiosyncratic a lot of sleep patterns and practices that are, in fact, pretty mainstream.

What *are* our cultural beliefs and expectations surrounding children's sleep? Where do they come from? Are they realistic when considered alongside the science of children's sleep? These are the questions the first three chapters of the book explores.

The second section of the book looks at *why* night waking is such a big deal in our culture. It probes the sleep experts' views and how their ideas fit (or don't fit) with real parents' needs and experiences. It identifies and examines temperament as an essential, yet often overlooked, piece of the night-waking puzzle. It also looks at the way the experience and attitudes of earlier generations color our perceptions of kids' sleep, in spite of all that has changed.

The final chapters of the book are all about coping. One takes us from Africa to Appalachia to Japan in an effort to uncover other cultures' customs and sleep strategies and to show, once and for all, that there is no one "right" way to manage children's sleep. Another offers a kind of manifesto to ease stressed-out parents' psyches. And perhaps most practical, the final chapter is chock full of parents' sleep solutions—almost fifty of them. You can't possibly walk away without some new inspiration.

B y now you know that you are holding a different kind of sleep book. It's not going to sell you one single approach to handling night waking. Parents—and children—are all different, and nighttime strategies need to fit individual moms, dads and kids to be successful.

This book is not going to compound your problem (if you see it as a problem at all) by adding a hefty load of guilt onto your fatigue and frustration.

It's not going to imply that all babies respond to training techniques or comforting strategies in about the same way when, in fact, the range of response is great.

What *is* it going to do?

It's going to address, head on, the complex tangle of factors that make night waking so tough on parents. It's going to acknowledge—embrace even—the differences between children and their parents, and the way that these differences shape nighttime experiences. It's going to offer strategies and ideas—not imperatives—that respect your ability to make wise choices for your family.

It's going to stake new ground by leaving you feeling better, not worse, after reading it.

2 A Sleepy Baby Is a Good Baby

I've had roughly the same conversation dozens of times since I became a parent eight years ago. It goes something like this. Grocery-store clerk or flight attendant or letter carrier or librarian: "Oh, what a sweet baby!"

Me, beaming: "Thanks."

"What's his name?"

"Jamie," or later, "Leo."

"He's so cute."

Me, nodding happily: "Yeah. Thanks."

"Is he good, too?"

Me, no longer nodding happily: "What do you mean?"

"Well, does he sleep through the night?"

This exchange puzzles me as much now, when 14-month-old Leo is the one burying his face in my shoulder, as it did when my grade-schooler, Jamie, was little. By asking what, exactly, the hapless stranger means by "good," I'm not being coy or evasive. I honestly don't get it, and keep hoping someone will be able to explain how a baby, as pure and close to absolute goodness as a person gets, can possibly be bad. And each time I'm reminded that, when it comes to kids, the mixed-up world tends to equate restfulness with goodness, I'm freshly dismayed.

Sleep myths permeate our parenting culture and color our perception of night waking. They loom over our shoulder in the middle of the night, whispering judgments about our competence or our child's future well-being. They muddy the issue by adding emotional and moral layers to what is essentially a practical problem.

Through the *Today's Parent* Sleep Survey, we learned a lot about the tall tales that really try parents' patience. Here are the mythical beasts that seem to rear their ugly heads again and again, and the evidence—both anecdotal and scientific—that lays them to rest.

Myth: A sleepy baby is a good baby

The good baby myth that has followed me around since I first gave birth is not just silly or annoying. It can also be detrimental to the fledgling relationship between a new infant and her caregivers.

Think about it: What is more important to moms and dads, more central to the task of parenting, than raising a good child? And yet, it takes only a few exchanges with tsk-tsking strangers before parents, who once saw their 3-month-old's small-hour summons as a sign of hunger or loneliness or vulnerability, begin to wonder if that crying isn't more cunning, somehow. They start to fret about being manipulated by a *baby*. And there you have it—parent and baby on opposite sides.

Yet you only have to pull at one thread of this argument to make the whole weave unravel. Saying that a "good" baby is one who sleeps through the night implies that the sweet little creature *chooses* to sleep through, whereas a not-good baby (I can't bring myself to even write "bad" in front of "baby") *chooses* to wake up. But in a way, these assumptions about night waking give babies way too much credit. As world-renowned child psychologist and parenting author Penelope Leach says in *Your Baby & Child*, "This kind of waking used to be called a 'bad habit': babies were ignored when they woke or even scolded or smacked to 'break the habit.' But babies cannot wake themselves on purpose. How can your baby learn not to do something which is outside his conscious control?" During a 1999 interview with *Today's Parent*, Leach went on to point out that *nobody*, not even adults, can purposely do—or not do—anything when he or she is asleep.

Although this myth is based on an obvious lapse in logic, most parents respond to hearing their child called "good" (or, by implication, "bad") on an emotional rather than an intellectual level. For the parent of a night waker, these casual words can sting like a slap. Tirsa Thompson explains: "As a first-time mom I have realized that friends, relatives and strangers gauge how well behaved or 'good' your child is by whether he sleeps through the night. I think parents, especially first-time parents, often beat themselves up over their ability to be a good parent. You don't want people to think you don't know what you are doing."

The question "Is your baby good?" isn't always about sleep. Independent nighttime behavior is just a single (though large) slice of the good-baby pie. But the other pieces—behaviors like long naps, patience in the mall, and quiet airplane conduct—don't have anything to do with true goodness, either. Since people insist on saying "good" when they really mean "easy," I guess the perfect child would require as little effort as a deep-dish dessert from the grocery store.

We seem to live in a culture that prefers children who get in the way of adults as little as possible. But that value isn't necessarily shared by the average mom or dad. Many of our sleep survey respondents stated passionately that although their children are not particularly easy to care for, they are definitely good, as well as "wonderful," "amazing" and "incredible."

Myth: Babies who don't sleep through the night are abnormal

If your baby is still waking beyond his half-birthday and you manage to escape feeling that's he's just plain bad, someone is probably going to tell you that he's not normal. Experts like Boston-based pediatrician and sleep clinician Richard Ferber have probably done more than anyone to soak this idea deep into our culture. In his bestselling *Solve Your Child's Sleep Problems* he writes, "You may not recognize that your child even has a problem, or...that the problem he does have should be considered a disorder that can and should be treated."

But if this were true, 62 percent of the respondents to the *Today's Parent* Sleep Survey would have babies with sleep disorders. That's the percentage of parents who said their little ones didn't start to sleep through the night until at least 8 months of age. More than 200 parents (about 16 percent) said their children were over a year old—in some cases, they were over 2 before the night waking stopped.

And then there are all the kids who fall into one of Ferber's other problem categories. "Symptoms...of possible sleep abnormalities which should be identified and treated are: frequent difficulty falling asleep at bedtime, waking during the night with inability to go right

---

SLEEP SURVEY STATS

Out of a total 1,484 respondents, 30 percent (445 respondents) reported having children aged 9 months or older who did not sleep through the night at survey time.

The remaining 1,039 parents were asked when their child began sleeping consistently through the night:

- 29% said their child was less than 4 months of age
- 27% said 4–7 months
- 20% said 8–12 months
- 10% said 13–18 months
- 6% said 19–24 months
- 8% said their child was over 2 years old

---

back to sleep alone, waking too early or too late in the morning, falling asleep too early or too late in the evening, or being irritable or sleepy during the day." That's just about everyone, isn't it?

Perhaps, then, the problem is not with our kids, but with our definition of "normal." That's what infant sleep researcher and anthropologist James McKenna thinks. "Data collected exclusively on the solitary sleeping, bottle-fed infant continue to provide the basis for definitions of and research into 'normal' infant sleep-wake patterns," he points out in his chapter on childhood sleep biology in the prestigious medical text, *Sleep and Breathing in Children and Pediatrics.* "These data continue to serve as the gold standard against which, eventually, parents and professionals evaluate infant sleep development," McKenna writes.

In other words, the babies in the *Today's Parent* survey "community," 75 percent of whom are breastfed, and 83 percent of whom sleep in their parents' bed at least occasionally, are being judged against babies who always sleep alone in their cribs and are bottle-fed.

Sure, these variables seem significant in theory, but do they make a difference in real life? You bet. Just consider Michele Crocker's experience. "Night waking was never an issue with our bottle-fed, slept-in-his-own-crib firstborn," she says. "He slept through the night until he grew out of his crib.

"When our daughter was born, we tried to fit her into the same mold without success. Luckily, she nursed, but it also meant frequent night waking. I was a zombie during the day because we had her in a crib and when she woke I would have to wake up, go to her room, sit on the edge of the bed or in a rocking chair until she was done. I was losing a lot of sleep."

Myth: A child's sleep habits reflect her parents' competence

Here is the flip side of the good-babies-sleep-through-the-night myth. If your baby is waking up at night, and there's nothing wrong with her, there must be something wrong with *you*.

In *Healthy Sleep Habits, Happy Child*, author Marc Weissbluth states outright what many sleep experts imply: "All children can learn to sleep well. The learning process will occur as naturally as learning how to walk. The bad news is that *parents* create sleep problems." (Italics his.)

Ferber seems to think so, too. In *Solve Your Child's Sleep Problems*, he says, "If your child is a restless sleeper or can't seem to settle down at night, you should be very careful about assuming that he is just a poor sleeper or doesn't need as much sleep as other children of the same age....I have found that almost all of these children are potentially fine sleepers and with just a little intervention can learn to sleep well." In other words, if parents just knew what they were doing, there would be no such thing as "poor" sleepers.

This insidious assumption has penetrated even confident parents' psyches. Although Sonja Whitchurch is a self-assured mother of two, she lapses into confessional mode when she discusses 10-month-old Molly's sleep habits. "I will admit the night sleeping is probably a lot our fault. When Molly was little, I was too tired (and too lazy) to stay up with her, plus it was winter and cold, so I would just bring her back to bed and nurse her, and we would go back to sleep within minutes."

Sonja talks about this nighttime routine as though it were a guilty secret. But McKenna would argue that Sonja is simply doing what comes naturally, and that what comes naturally is, in fact, highly evolved behavior that for thousands of years has met the needs of mothers and babies both. It is at once practical and humane.

So why the guilt? Because Sonja can't help but feel inadequate about Molly's night waking, or her approach to it. Although she has plenty of evidence to the contrary—Molly's obvious comfort with the arrangement, her older child's sound sleep habits in spite of early night waking, her own powerful instincts—Sonja's judgment is colored by what others think. And they think she's messing up. "I am so tired of people giving me advice on how to get her to sleep," she says.

On the other hand, having a baby who does manage on his own at night seems to indicate good parenting. As Brenda Blancher puts it, "Before we had a baby, we spent a lot of time listening to friends' talk of their children and there seemed to be a great deal of parental pride in a baby who slept through the night. It was like 'Hey, we know what we're doing, our baby sleeps all night.' I suppose I internalized these messages and when my son came along, I saw sleeping all night as one of the major milestones of development."

There are two issues here: One is the assumption that what a parent does or doesn't do determines a child's nighttime habits. Granted, a parent's response to night waking will, at some point, affect its duration and frequency. But consider this: Some 22 percent of our sleep survey respondents reported that their babies slept through the night at less than 4 months of age. However, less than 7 percent said they used a sleep-training method (see page 52) with babies in this age group. That means that most of these accommodating little ones started to sleep through the night spontaneously. Their parents didn't do anything right or wrong. They just, as one well-rested mom marvels, "really lucked out."

The second issue is about choice. It's about the choice parents make when they adopt an approach to night waking. Some moms and dads make that decision based on a dire need for quiet, undisturbed sleep. If they make silent nights a top priority, they may well succeed in getting their baby to sleep through. For other parents, uninterrupted sleep is a profound desire, but it's farther down on the "must do" list. In that case, parents may work hard at getting their child to sleep through the night. But like the Whitchurchs, they won't do it at all costs. "We tried several methods of sleep training, like the let-her-cry-it-out method with checking in at intervals," remembers Sonja. "Molly cried one night for over two hours, and was soaked in sweat, hysterical and managed to throw up she cried so much. We felt so guilty, we couldn't do it."

Is a parent who decides to call it quits after two hours of crying incompetent? Or is she appropriately matching her response to her child's needs, and to her beliefs about parenting in general?

Myth: Sleep training will work for every baby

Sleep training books give the impression that all babies will respond to training methods in more or less the same way. Ferber, for example, says, "The most common problem—sleeplessness in young children, has proven to be the easiest to treat. Even an infant or toddler who has never slept through the night can be doing so within a few days with the right assistance from parents." Similarly, on the back cover of *Teach*

Your Baby to Sleep Through the Night by Charles Schaefer and Michael Petronko, it says, "If you've had enough sleepless nights, read on—a good night's sleep is just a few days away!"

But parents like Amanda Knox beg to differ. "Before my son was born, I strongly believed in doing what worked for everyone else, as that must be what is right for my child. Aerik taught me a valuable lesson: every child is different."

That's why parents may find sleep training straightforward with one child and anything but with another. Says Catherine Barnes, "[My] oldest child was a good sleeper and responded to Ferber almost immediately. [My] second child is much more stubborn and could cry for two to three hours in the middle of the night."

Many other parents surveyed shared similar stories. Some described how they tried sleep training believing that yes, the first two or three nights would be exhausting, but then, peaceful nights would be theirs. Instead, these moms and dads found that the fifth and sixth nights were no better than the second, and a lot worse than their nights pre-training. Others chose the "controlled crying" with check-ups at regular intervals method, because they thought it less harsh than going cold turkey, but discovered that after each "reassuring" visit, their child became even more upset. (See page 52, Sleep Training: The Nutshell.) Still others found that sleep training worked the way it was supposed to—but only until their child's next asthma attack or ear infection, when ignoring their little one's distress was out of the question.

But there's another way that sleep training can fail. It has less to do with a child's response to the method and more to do with his parents' feelings. Karen Johnson puts it this way: "I tried to let my son cry himself to sleep because of other people's desires. When I was listening to Kyle cry, every instinct told me this wasn't right. This is not an issue of whether or not the method will work to enable my son to sleep, but rather, why would I ignore my son when he needs me?"

As Karen points out, an effective approach to sleep has to do more than "work." Experts don't seem to recognize what's plain to parents: A training method cannot be considered successful unless they feel good—or at least OK—about using it.

Myth: Night waking is harmful for children

Perhaps if parents were positive that night waking did nothing to hurt their kids, they would be easier on themselves. But by claiming either that it inhibits independence or that it interferes with proper rest, many sleep experts lead us to believe that night waking is bad for children.

Prominent pediatrician T. Berry Brazelton makes the independent sleep argument in his 1992 book, *Touchpoints*: "Being able to manage alone at night helps a child develop a positive self-image and gives her a real feeling of strength."

Joanne Cuthbertson and Susanna Schevill make a similar case in *Helping Your Child Sleep Through the Night*: "A child who depends on her parent's presence to sleep through the night cannot be as secure as the child who has learned to feel comfortable with herself."

But James McKenna doesn't buy it. He points out that since nobody has ever systematically studied the relationship between infant/child personality characteristics and sleep arrangements, conventional beliefs about independence and independent sleep are "misleading at best." On the other hand, he says there is some recent research that contradicts the independence myth.

Parents who allow their children to join them in bed when they wake, or who have a full-time family bed, are about as far as you can get from the independent sleep approach. So we might expect them to have the *most* dependent, screwed-up kids. But the research doesn't bear this out.

In 1994, Paul Heron, a researcher at the University of Bristol in England, studied the sleeping habits of middle class English children. He found that children who "never" slept in their parents' bed were harder to control, less happy and had more tantrums. He also found that children who were never permitted to climb into bed with their parents were *more* fearful than children who always slept in their parents' bed.

In a similar study, Heron found that the solitary sleeping children were harder to handle (as reported by their parents), dealt less well with stress and were rated as being more (not less) dependent on their parents than the co-sleepers.

So much for independent sleep as a cornerstone of child development. The other part of the "night waking is harmful" myth—that interrupted sleep is bad for children because it deprives them of rest—might just be Weissbluth's favorite refrain. In one of several ominous, bold-lettered paragraphs, he states: "You are harming your child when you allow unhealthy sleep patterns to evolve or persist—sleep deprivation is as unhealthy as feeding a nutritionally deficient diet."

Now, nobody would argue that true sleep deprivation is good for children (see page 31). But the verbal sleight of hand that equates waking intermittently at night with clinical sleep deprivation would be laughable, if it didn't hit parents so squarely where they are vulnerable. (Weissbluth's own method seems to invite more serious sleep deficits. Although he later modified his stand, in the first edition of his book, he advocated leaving babies to cry alone in their cribs for up to three or four hours!)

Remember that all young babies get the sleep they need in broken stretches around the clock. As we will see in the next chapter, the process of turning these "little sleeps" into a long one and a couple of daytime naps is gradual; it doesn't happen overnight. There is no obvious reason why an older baby, given ample opportunity to nap in the day, would suffer sleep deprivation because of night waking.

Myth: Sleeping with a baby is bad (for baby)

Because climbing into bed with a baby is taboo in our culture, there is a web of myths that surround the practice. After all, there needs to be a reason why you shouldn't sleep with your child, even if that reason is based in fiction rather than fact.

The most obvious and public concern is for physical safety. Claims about the dangers of co-sleeping have been around at least since the Middle Ages, when "accidental" overlying—the parent rolling over and suffocating the baby—was sometimes a last resort for families with too many little mouths to feed. But cultural anthropologists like Meredith Small point out that until 200 years ago, all babies slept with adults. And in her book *Our Babies, Ourselves*, Small explains that a great number of the world's babies still sleep with at least one adult. It is only in North America and parts of Europe (the same places where society highly values independent sleep for babies and private pillow time for

---

IS YOUR CHILD SLEEP-DEPRIVED?
Most babies and young children will make up for a rough night by napping longer, or by sleeping more the following night. And as we'll see in the temperament chapter, some children confound their parents by simply needing significantly less sleep than expected. Let your instincts, your child's behavior and his overall well-being be your guides. If he doesn't seem like himself, or if you are concerned that his lack of sleep is affecting his health, don't hesitate to check with your doctor.

---

parents) that people believe it's easy to crush a baby in bed. "The simple evidence that most babies around the world today sleep with a parent and they are not dying from suffocation should be enough to convince parents that it is pretty difficult to roll over on a baby and not notice," Small writes.

It should be enough, but it's not, especially now that a governmental agency has come out with a recommendation against bedding down with baby. In the fall of 1999, the United States' Consumer Product Safety Commission (CPSC) made its announcement. "Don't sleep with your baby or put your baby down to sleep in an adult bed," CPSC chairwoman Ann Brown stated.

Why not? The CPSC reported that 515 American children under two years of age died in standard adult beds, waterbeds and daybeds between 1990 and 1997. Three hundred and ninety four of these deaths were caused when the baby became trapped face-down or wedged between the mattress and the frame. The rest—121—were attributed to overlying. So although the CPSC's main message addressed the risk of overlying, many more tragedies were caused by what we already know to be dangerous: putting an infant down to sleep on a sagging mattress, a waterbed, a sofabed, or leaving a baby alone in an adult bed.

And what about the 121 deaths attributed to overlying? Co-sleeping advocates like McKenna maintain that people don't roll onto their babies unless they are drunk or stoned. He offers the following example: "In recent years in Cook County, Illinois (Chicago), the medical examiner has found that *all* overlying deaths were in situations in which the adult was intoxicated with either alcohol or illegal drugs." The CPSC's study, however, failed to isolate the condition of the parents as a factor in the cause of death. It also failed to mention that medically, death from "overlying" or suffocation looks just like SIDS (sudden infant death syndrome, in which an apparently healthy baby inexplicably dies while sleeping). Coroners say they really can't distinguish. So some of these "overlying deaths" may well have been caused by SIDS. The baby's being in an adult bed could have been incidental.

In addition, the CPSC laid its alarming message on parents without context. It didn't, for example, mention that these 515 deaths, measured over an eight-year period (that's fewer than 100 deaths a year), represent a tiny proportion of the 3.9 million babies born each year in the U.S. Nor did the report compare the number of babies who died in adult beds to the total number of babies who died in their sleep. But this information is significant: In 1997 alone, 2,705 babies died of SIDS in the U.S.

The bottom line? Most SIDS babies die while sleeping alone in their cribs. McKenna says, "Solitariness may conspire with infantile deficits to increase SIDS risk." In other words, if you take reasonable safety precautions, your baby is no more likely—and possibly even less likely—to die in your bed than she is in her own.

But safety concerns are only the tip of the iceberg. Deeper down lurks the conviction that bringing a baby into your bed is risky business, psychologically.

Ferber, for example, writes, "Sleeping in your bed can make your child feel confused and anxious rather than relaxed and reassured....If you allow him to crawl in between you and your spouse, in a sense separating the two of you, he may feel too powerful and become worried." If, on the other hand, "you take the easy way out and allow your child into your bed while one of you moves into his...he is literally replacing one of you in your bed as the other's partner. He may begin to worry that he will cause the two of you to separate, and if you ever do he may feel responsible."

Hold on a minute. How can an infant of just a few months of age possibly know enough about your former sleeping arrangements to have any concept of "separating the two of you?" And if he did, would he then have the capacity to worry about it? Where is Ferber's proof? The studies McKenna cites suggest that co-sleeping has the opposite effect. In a survey of college-age subjects, researchers found that men who slept with their parents between birth and age five had significantly higher self-esteem and experienced less guilt and anxiety. Another study, says McKenna, reported a similar finding for women. And if sleeping with parents makes kids anxious and neurotic, how do children from Japan to Guatemala manage to grow up unscathed?

Myth: Sleeping with a baby is bad (for adults)

Even if the kids are OK, bringing your baby into bed is, supposedly, bad for *you*. Ferber writes, "We know for a fact that people sleep better alone in bed." Perhaps, but only if they don't have to jump out of bed several times a night to attend to a crying child. Further, we have to look, again, at priorities. If a perfect night's rest were the chief objective of the average parent, and she accepted Ferber's statement, she wouldn't sleep with her partner, either. And Ferber certainly thinks *that's* important.

In fact, under the surface, this taboo against bed-sharing is *mostly* about sex. In our culture, beds and sex and sleep tend to be so inextricably linked that many people feel there's something inappropriate— perverted even—about bringing a child under the covers.

When Ferber claims that even a young toddler may find sleeping in your bed "overly stimulating," he's talking about sex. (This passage of his book, in the index, falls under the term "Sexual arousal.") He's more direct when voicing his view of co-sleeping as a form of sexual avoidance: "If there is tension between parents," he writes, "then taking a child into their bed may help them avoid confrontation and sexual intimacy." Winnipeg pediatrician Stan Lipnowski seems more permissive when he is quoted in a magazine article on independent sleep as saying, "It boils down to a matter of choice," but then he continues, "something else will have to be sacrificed, such as marital intimacy or conjugal duties."

Klaus Minde, former chairman of child psychiatry at McGill University and a sleep expert, is less carefully gender-neutral. In a draft chapter ("Sleep Disorders in Infants and Young Children") slated to appear in a professional text, he writes, "Mothers [with marital conflicts] often join their children in their beds at night because they prefer to sleep with them rather than with their spouses. Others will allow their 4-year-old to breast feed in public or be so 'intuned' to his emotional needs that they have few or no resources left for other members of their family." Namely, their husbands.

Minde and the others seem to be worried about kids intruding on their dads' conjugal rights—whether that means discouraging a woman from offering her breast to her child for "too long," or ensuring that she remain available (and undistracted) in the bedroom.

But let's get real: Most people, dedicated co-sleepers or not, realize that a family bed doesn't create a family den of iniquity. And although some parents *do* find it harder to be intimate with a little one in their bed, co-sleeping doesn't have to mean doing without. It just means loosening the link between the sack and sex.

Myth: Sleeping with a baby is always better

It's ironic: While many parents are made to feel guilty for responding to or sleeping with their night-waking babies, others feel guilty because they don't. The voice in favor of the family bed is not nearly as loud, but it can be very adamant. Pediatrician William Sears, for example, an advocate of "night-time parenting" and "sharing sleep," tries hard to maintain a flexible tone in *The Baby Book*, yet he occasionally succumbs to guilt-inducing phrases like, "How can the hands-off approach do anything but weaken your bond?"

In certain circles, weaning an older baby off nighttime feedings, letting a baby cry for any length of time or simply putting the baby to sleep in a separate room may be looked at as a form of abandonment. Insecurity, lack of trust, a poor parent-child relationship and teen violence may be the darkly anticipated outcomes. The specter of emotional damage is a powerful guilt trip, indeed.

Let's be clear: all kinds of happy, healthy, affectionate children slept alone in their crib as babies. All kinds of caring, skillful parents decide that it's worth a little bit of crying to teach a baby to sleep more independently. While we go to some lengths in this book to demonstrate that it's *OK* to sleep with your baby, nurse her in the night or get up with her as often as you can stand, we don't mean to imply that you have to, or even should, do these things. There are many possible "right" approaches to this thorny problem.

The point is to find the one that's right for you.

3 Sleep Cycle Logic

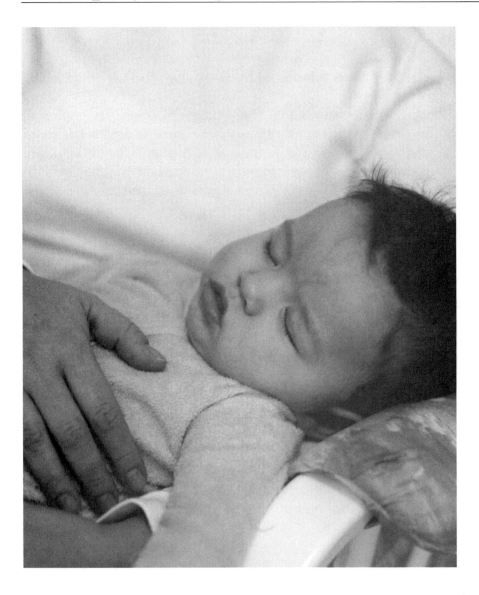

On cloudless nights, the moon shines into Leo's bedroom, lighting up a square of wall above his crib. Bedtime begins with him in my arms, leaning over to touch those moonbeams. "Goodnight moon," I say. Sometimes he gives a little wave. Then we get down to it.

When we begin to rock and nurse, my baby is lucid and wide-eyed. Ten or 15 minutes go by before his lids become heavy. Soon they're narrowing to a close each time the chair swings backwards. But they creep open again when we rock forward. He is drowsy, drifting, relaxed. His head is heavy in the crook of my arm, his toes uncurled. This is what sleep experts call Stage I.

The moon is higher when Leo's big brown eyes disappear completely behind translucent lids. If a dog barks or the rocker scrapes against a leg of the crib, his eyes snap open. Otherwise, they remain shut. His nursing continues to make me feel like a rug under a vacuum cleaner. By now he has probably entered sleep Stage II.

Next his breathing starts to change from short irregular puffs to deeper rises and falls. There will be three or four of these, and then he will shift a little bit in my arms, breathe more shallowly, make a tiny noise. If I try to extract my breast from his mouth, he resists or roots around like a newborn, without opening his eyes. He has moved into Stage III.

The heavy breathing becomes a constant pattern. I count to 40 or 50 before I try to break free. This time, he lets me. Leo's breathing becomes more shallow, but only for a moment. I shift in the rocking chair, then stand up with him heavy in my arms. I wait a little longer before I try to lay him in the crib. If I am successful, I can be pretty sure my baby has entered Stage IV.

Leo will cycle through these four levels of non-REM sleep for the rest of the night. He will also experience intermittent periods of REM sleep.

But if I want to observe this stage, characterized by rapid eye movement (hence the acronym REM) and associated with dreaming, I have to stick around for a while. Experts say he probably won't enter this more active sleep phase until he has gone through one or two non-REM cycles—each of which lasts about an hour.

As it is, I put the side of the crib up and tiptoe out of Leo's room to put away the dinner dishes, pack my 8-year-old's lunchbox and read the newspaper before entering Stage I myself.

Since I don't have the sophisticated equipment researchers use to measure sleep stages in my home, I'm guessing my way through Leo's descent into deep slumber. Still, these guesses are educated by sources like "What We Know About Sleep," the most scientific chapter in Ferber's *Solve Your Child's Sleep Problems*, and Klaus Minde's article "The Sleep of Infants and Why Parents Matter." These models show the way that "sleep architecture" changes and develops throughout a child's life.

The Young and the Restless: Understanding Newborn Sleep

Although sleep patterns vary with the individual, newborn sleep is markedly different from that of older babies, children and adults. For one thing, a newborn enters REM sleep immediately after dozing off instead of descending first through non-REM Stages I through IV. (For more on sleep stages, see page 45.) The terminology is different too: For infants, REM sleep is referred to as Active Sleep and non-REM as Quiet Sleep.

Active Sleep is characterized by twitches, irregular breathing, eye movement under translucent eyelids, and those fleeting little newborn smiles. During Quiet Sleep, a baby will breathe deeply and lie very still. She might make sucking motions and may, occasionally, startle with a sudden body movement. Brain waves during Quiet Sleep are also different from older children's. The slower waves that characterize the deep sleep stages occur in bursts rather than a continuous flow. Over the first four weeks or so, the non-REM brain waves become continuous, and babies startle less often. Non-REM sleep stages start to emerge during the second month. It is interesting to note that large, slow K-complex waves (see box page 45) don't appear until around 6 months of age.

Experts expect full-term newborns to spend 50 percent of their shut-eye in REM (Active) sleep—premature babies, 80 percent. A certain level of brain maturity is required for Quiet Sleep, and that's why sleep specialists see less of it in newborns. Also, many experts believe that REM sleep helps develop babies' brains. Clinicians have traditionally found that the amount of time a child spends in REM sleep decreases throughout childhood. By about 3 months of age, babies start to enter non-REM sleep first, and by 3 years of age, says Ferber, only 33 percent of a child's sleep is REM sleep. Adolescents spend only 25 percent of their sleep in REM, a level that remains constant into adulthood.

Typically, newborn slumber is made up of short periods of sleep mixed with shorter periods of wakefulness. Initially, these periods are arranged randomly over a 24-hour day. In fact, many parents swear that their babies confuse day and night, and sleep longer and deeper in the daytime than they do at night.

But when most infants are around three months of age, their brains begin to take in the difference between day (light) and night (dark), so they start to consolidate the shorter periods of sleep into longer ones. That's why the pressure on parents of night wakers usually intensifies around this time. "Most infants have settled, that is, they are now sleeping through most of the night" at around 3 months, says Ferber. "By six months almost all infants will have settled, and the continuous nighttime sleep has increased," he continues. "A typical baby of this age will sleep about 12 hours at night with only occasional brief wakings."

While few parents would argue that their 6-month-old does more of his sleeping during the day than at night, many would say that figuring out the difference between day and night does not automatically lead to *continuous* sleep.

Sleep research has shown that babies have shorter sleep cycles than adults. This makes a difference to night waking because all of us are most likely to wake in the night when we are moving between phases. (Shorter cycles = more cycles = more waking.) As kids grow, their sleep-cycle length increases but, surprisingly, the total amount of deep sleep (Stage IV) decreases. At least that's what sleep experts have long believed. However, newer research collected on breastfed babies and babies who sleep with their mom or dad (even part-time) shows that these "truths" are not carved in stone. While some aspects of children's sleep physiology may not be affected by feeding or sleeping arrangements, others definitely are.

Is There a Right Way to Fall Asleep?

Bedtime is only the beginning of our nightly routine with Leo. Anywhere from an hour to 2½ hours after nodding off, my son will wake, sit up in his crib and cry or call out. There are rare nights when Leo "forgets" to wake up, but the rest of the time, we respond promptly. My husband and I are long past trying to get our baby to go back to sleep on his own. Instead, Michael or I get him from his crib quickly and bring him into our bed.

Why does Leo wake up? Ferber explains that all children—all people, in fact—alternate between periods of lighter and deeper sleep each night. Many babies, he and other like-minded experts say, know how to sink from periods of light sleep or even wakefulness (Stages I and II) back into deeper sleep (Stages III and IV) without adult help. These little guys are called "self-soothers." But when a baby like Leo surfaces, Ferber says, he becomes aware that he is no longer where he was when he fell asleep—nursing, in my arms—so he cries out instead of drifting back into deeper sleep.

This is a matter of sleep associations, Ferber explains. If Leo connects parental attention with sleep, he will want to be with a parent each time he falls asleep. The solitary sleep guru sees this as a "severe sleep disturbance" and devotes a whole chapter of his book to sleep associations and the problems the wrong ones—like nursing—can cause.

However, infant sleep researcher James McKenna takes issue with Ferber's assertion that *putting* a baby like Leo to sleep, instead of leaving him to fall asleep on his own, is a mistake, and that the only way to deal with this "problem" is to break the association. "In Western cultures, clinicians continue to advocate only one form of sleep for infants (solitary sleep), and sleep management strategies aimed at sharply reducing as early in life as possible parental handling and feeding of infants at bedtime. Parents are encouraged not to permit infants to associate falling asleep with food (including breast-feeding) or parental touch. If falling asleep at the breast is as common and, apparently, as biologically appropriate as cross-cultural data suggest, then this recommendation will prove problematic for many mothers and infants."

And how. Although Ferber thinks that most young children associate falling asleep with "being in a particular bedroom, lying in a certain crib or bed and holding a favorite stuffed animal or special blanket," the *Today's Parent* Sleep Survey found that many little ones associate nodding off with holding mom or dad instead. So do children in myriad cultures around the world. (See Chapter 7 for a detailed look at sleep practices in other places.)

In this case, McKenna argues, the conventional model just doesn't apply. "The truth is that until recently, we knew little about infant or young children's sleep cycles, unless you believe that infants and children sleeping alone, weaning early, bottle feeding and feeding little or not at all at nighttime represent the conditions under which the phenomenon is properly understood. If your baby will sleep alone and is bottle fed then the models shown in popular parenting books *may* be applicable."

Even then, McKenna says, it is important to remember that each child is an individual. "Your baby is different from every other and if his temperament or needs require touch and reassurance, the solitary model may not work."

Physiology may play a part, too, says McKenna. He contends that, from an evolutionary point of view, a young baby's night waking can be looked at as a kind of self-preservation. He and other anthropologists explain that humans are born neurologically unfinished—we are, in fact, the most underdeveloped of all the primates at birth. This means that navigating a sea of transitions between lighter and deeper sleep—when body temperature, breathing, heart rate and other functions have to slow down and speed up again, several times—is tricky for a little baby. There is always the danger that he will drift into a deep sleep and be unable to wake up, which is what seems to happen when infants die of sudden infant death syndrome.

Night waking looks like a natural (though partial) protection against this risk. Although it is generally assumed that neurological development "catches up" at 3 or 4 months of age, McKenna says, "I suspect that night waking may be more important for some babies than others right through the first year of life and that's why they wake up."

Synchronized Sleep

Back in my bedroom, Leo takes his place between Michael and me in our queen-sized bed. If I have not turned my light out already, this is a cue for me to do so. Bracing his tiny feet against my thigh, my baby grabs a handful of my T-shirt, turns to face me and nurses himself back to sleep. It's funny—no matter how awake I was before Leo's arrival, I usually start to drift off at this point.

That would make perfect sense to McKenna, who has done three studies comparing co-sleeping and solitary sleeping mother-infant pairs at the Sleep Disorders Lab at Irvine's University of California. If McKenna were to wire up Leo and me the way he does subjects in his lab, he'd surely witness the same phenomenon that has fueled the ground-breaking sleep research that has made him famous: a remarkable parallel in "sleep architecture" when moms and babies sleep together.

In each of McKenna's studies, mothers' and infants' brain wave signals, eye movements, respiration, cardiac beats and muscle tone were measured while they slept. In addition, an infrared video camera taped movements of mother and child throughout the night, so that McKenna and his colleague, Sara Mosko, could track the pairs qualitatively and quantitatively.

McKenna and Mosko found that co-sleeping mothers and their babies are as biologically entwined when asleep as they are emotionally connected when awake. Every time the polygraph machine (yes, this is what we usually think of as a lie detector) recorded a change in a mother's brain waves, her baby responded with his own shift in brain activity. Similarly, when an infant's heart rate or respiration signaled his movement from one sleep stage to another, his mom, though not conscious, protectively went along with him. This dance is so finely choreographed that the pairs moved together through even transient arousals—when one or the other surfaced for just a moment, and then went back into a deeper sleep.

That's amazing enough, especially when you consider that a solitary sleeping baby's sleep cycle length—the amount of time between two consecutive appearances of the same sleep stage—is about an hour, while adults typically take 90 minutes to traverse the same ground. But that's not all. The sleep scientists' videotapes show that mothers and babies usually end up facing each other in sleep, even if they aren't arranged that way at bedtime. In addition, co-sleeping mothers exhibited nurturing behavior throughout the night: The tapes showed that moms repeatedly touched and cuddled their babies, adjusting covers and positioning, even when the polygraph clearly indicated that they were asleep.

Finally, McKenna and Mosko found that when little ones spend the night next to mom, they sleep differently than they do alone. This held true even for the infants in the study who were used to sleeping solo. Specifically, they sleep more lightly, spending more time in Stages I and II, and less in the heavier Stages III and IV. They also exhibit more REM sleep than other babies their age. These findings are significant not just in and of themselves, but also in relation to safe sleep for young babies. As Meredith Small, author of *Our Babies, Ourselves*, says in her description of McKenna's work: "Each time the baby responds to an arousal by its mom, an extra arousal from the baby's point of view, the response sets in motion a cycle that gives infants additional practice in breathing."

"Most nights I don't mind waking with my baby as our sleep rhythms seem to have meshed."
—*Terri Orlando, mother of three*

McKenna and Mosko's research shows that the tranquilizing effect Leo has on me when he comes to snooze by my side may be physiological as well as psychological. As my co-sleeping partner, Leo's mere presence, as well as his sleep-altered breathing, heart rate and other bodily functions, probably cues my own system to start shutting down for the night.

This work solves a couple of other puzzles, too. For example, it explains why I, like the moms in their studies, find the nights I spend with Leo *less* tiring than the occasional nights when he sleeps in his crib till 3 or 4 a.m., even though I probably wake more often when he's with me. One reason is pretty straightforward: I don't have to get out of bed to care for him. In fact, like the mothers on the videotapes, I don't even have to fully wake up. But even when I do, I rarely experience that impossibly thick, difficult-to-think feeling that sudden waking can

THE FIVE STAGES OF SLEEP

STAGE 1: This is the stage of drowsiness. Your child's awareness of the external world starts to dim.

STAGE II: Your child is asleep, but he is easily wakened. Often when adults wake after being in Stage II, they do not believe that they were asleep. On a polygraph, this stage is characterized by short bursts of very rapid brain wave activity (called sleep spindles). Large slow waves called K-complexes also begin to appear.

STAGES III AND IV: Your child is more deeply asleep. The smaller and faster brain waves of light sleep and waking disappear, and now the polygraph shows mostly large, slow swells called delta waves. His breathing and heart rate become very stable. By Stage IV, it is very difficult to wake him. Simply calling your child's name is likely to wake him from Stage II, but he would probably be oblivious by Stage IV.

REM SLEEP: An entirely different state, associated with dreaming. When your child is experiencing REM sleep, both his breathing and heart rate become irregular. His reflexes, kidney function and pattern of hormone release change. His brain waves will become quite active again, showing a mixture of waking and drowsy patterns. "The mind now wakes," says Ferber, "but the wakefulness of the dream state is quite different from that of true waking." Your child responds mainly to signals originating within his own body instead of from the world around him. Sleep experts suspect that the characteristic eye movements of this state result from the sleeper watching his dreams occur.

cause. Moving through the various stages of sleep in tandem means that when Leo does wake, I'm near waking myself. Similarly, my deep sleep is less likely to be disturbed when Leo is close by, because at those (few) times of the night when I'm completely unplugged, he probably is, too. (Interestingly, sleep scientists believe a good night's sleep doesn't depend on spending any particular amount of time at any given sleep stage. Feeling rested, it seems, has more to do with the number of sleep cycles traversed overnight.)

Another little mystery McKenna's work unravels: According to Ferber's model, babies spend more of their sleep time in Stage IV (deep sleep) than older children. But this doesn't wash with my own experience, nor with the experiences of many survey respondents. When I go into my 8-year-old's bedroom at night, I can adjust his covers, touch him, even roll his 60-pound body over if he's too close to the edge of the bed, and he will not wake up. My 1-year-old, on the other hand, seems to sleep with one eye open. When I put him down in his crib, I have to make absolutely sure I don't forget anything in his room, because just the squeak of the floorboards when I re-enter is often enough to wake him. This is the opposite of what you'd expect after reading Ferber. It seems that my baby should be the heavier sleeper, and my big boy the one who sleeps more lightly. If James hadn't been just as light a sleeper when he was a baby, I would chalk it all up to temperamental differences. Instead, McKenna's research has got me thinking that Leo really does sleep more lightly than Ferber expects him to, more lightly than his older brother, and more lightly than he will a few years from now. That's because he's breastfeeding.

Like bed-sharing, breastfeeding changes the way babies sleep. McKenna cites research showing that bottle-feeding leads to an increase in quiet sleep whereas breastfeeding babies sleep more lightly and wake more often as they move from stage to stage. As McKenna pointed out, the standard model is based on bottle-feeding, solitary-sleeping babies, so it doesn't take these factors into account. And yet, we often cling to this model. As a result, many parents who breastfeed, in addition to those who sleep even occasionally with their babies, end up bending themselves out of shape so that they can fit into the glass slipper of conventional sleep theory. Maybe it's time to forget the fairy tale and find a shoe that fits.

4 What the Experts Say

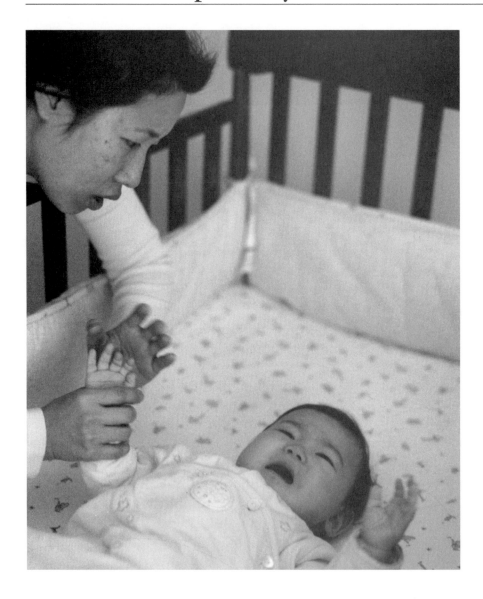

AND WHY IT'S NOT ENOUGH

The pediatrician is listening to Leo's breathing when he asks, "Is he sleeping through the night yet?" "No," I tell him. "Well then, time to let him cry," is his cheerful reply. I'm glad he's not looking at my face as he says this. "Honestly, it'll be fine," says the doctor while he checks my baby's ears. He knows this for certain, it seems.

He also knows that night waking is hard on parents, that pediatric sleep experts have found a "solution" and that he's never seen a child who seemed damaged by a little sleep training.

But here are a few things he doesn't know: My night table is crowded with books on kids' sleep; I've discussed the rights and wrongs of Ferberizing and the family bed with everyone from the local librarian to the Purolator man; I am completely and utterly unable to let my babies cry it out at night.

Of course, these passions boil beneath the surface. When Leo's doctor glances at me, I suspect that all he sees is a tired-looking mom. After seeing many tired moms, he has come to assume that we all want him to help us be less tired.

Yet there's more to mothers than our fatigue. Although I've known this man since my 8-year-old was born, although he has treated my kids for ear infections, eczema and chicken pox, he has no sense of my parenting style, nor my priorities. It's not that these are secret. They just haven't come up.

I don't really have the nerve to hash this out in the doctor's office, but I do have enough confidence to feel only fleeting self-doubt for the balance of the appointment. By the time I'm buckling Leo into his car seat, my feeling that my husband and I know what's best for both our kids—and for our family—has returned. Still, I crave reinforcement, so when we get home, I call up a friend who once complained of a similar experience with her child's doctor. Yup, we tell each other, there is more than one way to bring up baby.

A pediatrician is an expert on children's health. We respect him, maybe even revere him a little; we trust him to know what's right for our kids. But night waking is not a health problem. My 6-month-old, your 8-month-old and the countless other babies who wake up at night aren't sick; their night waking probably doesn't need to be treated with a medical prescription.

The Parent-Doctor Dynamic

Many of us have picked up a blueprint for interaction with doctors from our parents, or from our parents' generation overall. The last time I took my kids to see their grandparents, this became clearer than ever. On this particular visit, my mother-in-law dug something out of her drawer and put it in my hands. "Thought you might find this little book interesting," she said. Boy, did I. Given to her upon the birth of her first child—my husband—in 1967, *A Few Words About Babies* was a manual written and distributed by her pediatrician, Ralph Olsen.

Freely mixing medical fact with his own opinions, Olsen advised on everything from diapering ("plastic pants should probably be used only when visiting a wealthy relative who has to hold the baby") to the evils of commercially prepared baby food ("I certainly don't approve: a 2 oz jar of baby carrots costs 13 cents. Figuring half of that is water, you're paying $2.08 for a pound of carrots"). There were few areas that Olsen left to a parent's prerogative: He counselled on pet management and pacifier use, footwear and, yes, sleep ("I think the most common cause of babies being awake all night is a heavy blanket sleeper"). Some of his advice is no longer accurate (he told parents to put their babies down to sleep on their tummies; we now know that the danger of SIDS is greater when babies sleep this way), and some of it is quaint (13 cents for baby food!), but what is really fascinating is the tone in which it is all delivered. Reading this slim volume feels like a stern talking-to from your father.

So I consulted my mother-in-law. What did she think of Dr. Olsen's booklet? As a young mother, was there anything about it that put her off? Not at all. She found it helpful and was happy to follow Olsen's instructions without a second thought. She took for granted that when it came to baby care, he knew more than she did in every way. He was, after all, the expert.

The relationship today's parents have with their children's doctors has both evolved and stayed the same. Pediatricians still give all kinds of non-medical advice. And that, in itself, is a good thing. Doctors can be a dependable resource for parents. But that advice is still often presented as fact when it is closer to opinion. Perhaps most problematic, the advice tends to arrive with built-in assumptions about parents' priorities and lifestyle.

One Size Fits All?

My doctor and Ralph Olsen mean well, as do many of those who dole out one-size-fits-all sleep advice. There's no doubt about it: Pediatricians and sleep experts have helped lots of people—Theresa Howell, for example: "By two months, my son slept through the night on his own," she says. "It lasted only a week. So I figured if he could do it for a week, why not from then on? I started to let him cry for five minutes at a time. Then I would go in and reassure him that he was OK. This method only took me four days. He caught on and began sleeping through the night again. I did the same thing with my second son, and it only took him two days!"

But our survey reveals that many parents are not like Howell. Some struggle for weeks to train their babies, only to give up, frustrated, discouraged and more exhausted than ever. Others find sleep training so

SLEEP TRAINING: THE NUTSHELL

The sleep-training method that Boston-based pediatrician and sleep clinician Richard Ferber is famous for is by far the most well-known and widely used in North America. Basically, "Ferberizing" involves going through your bedtime routine, then putting your baby or child (the same basic method is given for both, with minor adjustments) to bed awake and leaving the room promptly—no additional rocking, nursing or back rubbing allowed. If he cries, you are to leave him for at first short and then longer intervals, until he eventually learns how to fall asleep on his own.

ON THE FIRST NIGHT, you are allowed to return to him after five minutes for a brief period of mutual reassurance. But you are not to pick him up. "Remember," says Ferber, "you are going in to reassure him and yourself, not necessarily to help him stop crying and certainly not to help him fall asleep. The goal is for him to learn to fall asleep alone without being held, rocked, nursed, or using a bottle or pacifier."

After this first visit, parents are to wait 10 more minutes before going back to their child for a second brief visit. This time, you are to wait 15 minutes, and if, after that time, the child is still crying "vigorously," you once again return to his room for a quick check. Fifteen minutes is the longest Ferber has you wait on the first night, so parents are to continue leaving their child to cry for 15 minutes between quick visits until he falls asleep during one of the intervals.

counter to their parenting instincts that night waking seems pleasant by comparison.

Consider Inga Ford's experience, for example. "Shortly after my son Storm's birth, on his first visit to his doctor, I was told that if he was not sleeping through the night by the time he was 3 months old, to let him cry himself back to sleep. My husband and I talked it over and immediately changed pediatricians. We were blessed to find one that had the same ideas on rearing children. We are under the belief that when a child awakens crying at night, he is in need of a little comforting. Comforting is something our children need as much as we as parents do."

If your child wakes in the night, the entire process is repeated for each awakening, so that at first parents wait just 5 minutes before going in for a quick check, then they wait 10 minutes, and finally, they go to 15 minutes and continue to check in with their child for however many 15-minute intervals it takes.

ON THE SECOND NIGHT, you are to wait 10 minutes before first going in to check on your child at bedtime or upon night waking. The second wait is 15 minutes, and the third and final interval for day two is 20 minutes. If the child is not asleep after the first 20-minute interval either at bedtime or during the night, parents are to continue to wait and check every 20 minutes until he falls asleep.

ON NIGHTS THREE THROUGH SEVEN, the time you are supposed to leave your child to cry is increased in 5-minute increments. So you wait 15 minutes to go in the first time on night three and work up to a maximum of 25 minutes, you wait 20 minutes to go in the first time on night four and work up to a maximum interval of a half hour, and so on. If you are still working on sleep training after seven nights (and Ferber seems to doubt that you will be), you wait 35 minutes before your first visit and work your way up to a maximum of 45 minutes for third and subsequent visits.

Clearly, Inga was even less receptive to her pediatrician's recommendation than I was. Why *do* some doctors insist on making night waking into a problem, even if parents don't feel that it is?

Joyce Barrett is a retired physician who focused her practice on pediatrics and obstetrics for almost 30 years. Here's her explanation: "Doctors are used to giving advice. We aren't trained to say, 'Hey, that is a common situation. What do *you* think—how do you want to handle it with your baby?' Because it isn't how we are trained, we don't do it, and because we don't do it, patients don't expect it. So they don't take our ideas as the start of a conversation or dialogue; they will often listen to our opinions—which may be very different from theirs—without arguing or commenting at all."

Sound familiar? Sometimes doctors are nudged into this role by anxious parents searching for answers. With our society's refusal to normalize night waking beyond the first few months, it's easy for a new parent to become seriously concerned (rather than simply but profoundly exhausted) when sleep doesn't come as expected.

Denise is one such mom. "When my daughter was born, I was full of expectations and hopes. The problem was, she decided that my hopes were not hers. She was constantly waking up from the beginning. She would be dead-to-the-world tired, limp as could be, and you would go to put her into her bed, and as soon as you put her down, ding, her eyes popped open. I talked repeatedly to our pediatrician about it. He kept saying, 'Leave her to cry, it will do her good. She will learn.' But she would cry and cry for hours."

Of course there is nothing wrong with Denise going to her child's doctor for advice, if that's what she wants to do; nor is he wrong to give it. But Denise needs to know that "leaving her to cry because it will do her good" is the doctor's *personal* opinion, not his *medical* opinion. She should feel free to take it or leave it. And her doctor has to remember that just because Denise—and 10 or 20 or 50 other parents—come in asking him what to do about night waking doesn't mean that all parents need to be told to let their baby cry it out. Some might find this advice helpful, but others will find it useless. Still others will discover that it does more harm than good, either because it causes the nighttime troubles to escalate, or because it leads them to doubt their own instincts as parents.

So doctors offer unsolicited advice for night waking because they assume it's what parents want—or need. But they don't always stop there. Some doctors push sleep training—from Ferber's controlled crying to Weissbluth's cold turkey—on parents. How come?

The Quick Fix

First of all, these methods often get at least partial results. Although sleep training doesn't always work, it definitely ranks as a quick fix. That means that instead of having to just listen and nod sympathetically when you talk sleep, your doctor can do what doctors do best: give you a remedy. "Do this in this way for three to five nights and you will be cured."

In addition, your doctor is going to be influenced by the sleep experts, most of whom are doctors themselves. Take Ferber, for example. He is both a sleep specialist and a pediatrician—perfect credentials, from another doctor's point of view. His approach seems solid, scientific and proven. And his book delivers the whole thing in a nutshell, which means that your doctor can recommend it, knowing it will be easy to read and simple to implement.

It's simple, all right. That's the problem. Ferber's book is so decisive, so free of ifs, ands or buts, that it fails, almost entirely, to take parents' styles, kids' temperaments and individual family circumstances into account.

Says Christine Plsapia: "The techniques outlined in books like Ferber's are great and work but mainly in a perfect world. How does one cope with the trauma of applying the techniques only to have to start over again after a setback caused by a week of asthma attacks suffered by the child? Also, how do two working parents cope with the rigorous techniques when they too need their sleep?"

Audrey Chan encountered an equally common set of disruptions: "We trained my son to sleep according to Ferber's method when he was 20 months old, but then went to Hong Kong for three weeks. When we came back we kept putting off the retraining and then I got pregnant and was too tired. Then he was out of the crib, which makes it even harder."

Manuals like Ferber's, based on cases seen in his clinic, imply that if these methods worked for families with major sleep problems, they will surely work for you. It seems to me they've got it backwards. It is precisely because these approaches were designed for troubled cases that they *don't* work for everyone.

An ordinary parent who picks up *Solve Your Child's Sleep Problems* because the title catches her eye, or because her doctor/mother/best friend recommends it, may merely be curious, or she may be damn sick and tired of night waking. But one thing is almost certain: She is not desperate the way a parent who pines for an appointment at a sleep clinic is. Whether her child's night waking is mildly inconvenient or a real drag, it probably isn't so problematic that it threatens her family life as a whole. If it were, *she* would be the one headed for the sleep clinic. In other words, night waking arouses a broad spectrum of parental feelings and stress levels, and this range gets ignored when strategies designed for people in real trouble are mass-marketed.

As a result, the solution can feel a lot worse than the problem. As Carrie Jones, a Calgary mom, explains: "I only mentioned in passing that Harris was still waking up at night when our family doctor urged me to get Ferber's book. He said the method really worked. What he didn't say was that 'the method' would turn our household upside down: It kept all of us—our two older kids too—up most of each night, it made us afraid to leave Harris with a sitter or vary his routine in any way, and it left me feeling simply awful about myself as a mother. I'm sure the method does work, but at what price?"

Tunnel Vision

This is what a friend of mine calls "the expert's tunnel vision," and the narrow focus blocks insight in two ways: First, the sleep specialist approaches kids' sleep with a crisis mentality. He gets used to seeing families for whom night waking *has* become a huge problem, a problem that might, perhaps, have been nipped in the bud with early sleep training. From these experiences he extrapolates, figuring that every family can benefit from a little preventative medicine, lest they become one of those troubled cases. But because he sees so many families in crisis and so few typical ones, he fails to recognize that most night waking is normal and will peter out, not worsen.

Secondly, the expert in any specialized field can become so focused on fixing the problem in his area of expertise that he loses sight of the whole child, or in a case like Jones's, the whole family. He (or she) seems to "forget" that unbroken sleep or perfect teeth or a balanced diet is not our sole objective in parenting. What good is it to get your baby sleeping through the night if you all become miserable people in the process?

In his book *Heathy Sleep Habits, Happy Child*, Marc Weissbluth

---

SURVEY STATS

We asked parents: "Which of the following experts' approaches to sleep have you read/heard of?"

- **74% had heard of Richard Ferber**
- **25% agreed with him**
- **51% had heard of William Sears**
- **28% agreed with him**
- **49% had heard of Penelope Leach**
- **21% agreed with her**
- **36% had heard of T. Berry Brazelton**
- **7% agreed with him**

---

provides a couple of classic examples of sleep-expert tunnel vision. For instance, he advocates very early bedtimes for *all* babies, toddlers and preschoolers. Urging parents to put their kids down for the night as early as 6:30 p.m., he flatly dismisses concerns about the way this might cut into family time. In fact, he feels that more flexible sleep routines are a sign of selfish parenting. Boxed and in bold letters he states: "Please don't think that it has no lasting effect when you routinely keep your child up too late for your own pleasure after work or because you want to avoid bedtime confrontations..." Weissbluth's idea of "too late"? A bedtime after 8 p.m.

A section on "Dual-Career Families" makes a similar point, this time in the form of a Q and A with a parent. The parent's question goes like this: "I miss my baby so much during the day, why can't I spend more time with her at night? The only time I have to love my baby is late at night. Won't she miss me?" Weissbluth sugarcoats his answer, but his message is clear. If you keep your child up "late," she will miss her sleep far more than she ever misses you. When he says "your baby's needs must come first," he is talking about sleep needs, and is overlooking a baby's intense need for a close, loving relationship with her parents.

Why does playing with your child in the evening have to mean "withholding sleep" anyway? In fact, many parents do put their children to bed outside of Weissbluth's strict 6 to 8 p.m. window without the dire consequences—like severe sleep deprivation and "children so overtired that they appear to be in pain"—that Weissbluth predicts. These families simply adapt their children's sleep schedules, by lengthening afternoon naps or allowing a later morning wake-up, to accommodate a connection time that is as important to the child emotionally as sleep is to her physically.

In their insistence on putting children's sleep requirements (or what they believe are children's sleep requirements) first, sleep specialists can be blind to the other needs in the family. The also give short shrift to the human relationships and personal circumstances that are the very essence of family life.

The Human Element

The medicalized, systematized approach to night waking has another drawback: it removes the human element. At a comfortable distance and on paper, experts prescribe a program that looks reasonable and appears to get results. However, they are not the ones who are emotionally and biologically cemented to that little human being, they are not faced with listening to someone they love so much in distress, they are not slogging through the whole damn thing at 3 a.m., so exhausted that they feel as though they were dragging around lead weights. Even when the experts mention these realities, they talk about them as though they were distractions that cloud parents' judgment, not legitimate factors that make a difference.

On a program that aired on Canadian public radio, Penelope Leach put it this way: "The [sleep] program idea worries me actually because I think sometimes it makes parents feel that they ought to do things that they aren't comfortable doing. . . . This idea that you have a sheet of paper all laid out in boxes for you, and you tick off the number of minutes you left your child crying or the number of times you went in or the number of this's and thats and the others that you did on the first night and the next night—it kind of makes a bit of a barrier between the reality of one small human being, lying in his crib crying, and one larger human being, standing out in the hall, sweating."

Sleep experts can learn something from mainstream health care, which has finally started to consider the way a person feels as equally significant to her medical test results. Perhaps this change is on its way. Family bed supporters have joined the ranks of the sleep experts. And in recently published interviews, Ferber himself has recanted some of his hard-line advice in favor of a more flexible model.

And yet, *Solve Your Child's Sleep Problems* is still prominent on the shelves, and in it Ferber still presumes to know what you want better than you do yourself. Consider the following passage:

> If you are in the habit of rocking your child to sleep for twenty to thirty minutes each night and getting up once or twice to rock him back to sleep in the middle of the night, you actually may be interfering with his sleep and postponing the start of his sleeping through the night. Even if you don't mind getting up, I suspect you would be happier if you could simply put him down at bedtime without rocking and have him sleep through the night as well.

Not so fast, Ferber. That's what his colleague Jack Newman would say. Also a pediatrician, Newman has recently penned *Dr. Jack Newman's Guide to Breastfeeding* along with co-author Teresa Pitman. In it, they write, "One of the great pleasures of parenthood, in my opinion, is having a baby fall asleep in your arms. It makes you feel good. It makes you feel competent. The little guy trusts me so much he will just fall asleep in my arms. And the heat he gives off when he just falls into sleep—what a pleasure it is to feel that. But too many parents are being advised to make sure this never happens, because this will be spoiling the baby and he will never sleep through the night. It is not true."

Mother Blame

Another problem arises when sleep experts fail to consider individual priorities and needs: They begin to see night waking as a sign of inept parenting, rather than the by-product of larger choices being made.

This became clear to me when I read a book chapter by psychiatrist and sleep expert Klaus Minde. In a forthcoming book called *Infant and Toddler Mental Health: Models of Clinical Intervention with Infants and Their Families,* Minde claims that bedtime and night waking difficulties are usually paralleled by problems in the "daytime interaction between child and caregivers." To learn about the parent-child relationship, says Minde, it is best to "observe the primary caregiver and the problem sleeper during a free play period.... This period does not need to exceed 10 minutes for reliable results." So according to Minde, after watching a caregiver and a toddler spend 10 minutes (10 minutes!) doing something like cleaning up blocks, it is possible to get to the root of the sleep problem.

Then he goes on to claim that poor sleepers and their caregivers are characterized by these kinds of difficulties: "The partners are not focused on the same activity or event; there is little verbal dialogue or turn-taking activity in which both partners are engaged in a mutually responsive way; the parent's and child's activity levels are poorly matched as are their moods; expressions of anger or excessive control appear in either child or caregiver during the play activities..."

But but but.... How can you measure dialogue when one of the partners is just learning to talk? How can you discuss sharing when one of the turn-takers is stuck in the "Mine!" stage? And how on earth can you expect the activity level of an adult to equal that of a toddler?

Still, he goes on. "The presence of...interactive difficulties suggests that the parent finds it hard to set age appropriate limits. This failure may have a specific motive (e.g., mother may like to have her infant for company in preference to her husband or as replacement during husband's absence) or it may be related to a past event in the mother's life." No, you are not missing something. Yes, we have gone directly from looking at the "interaction between child and caregiver" to mother using her baby to ward off her husband.

Alternatively, Minde explains, mothers might use their babies to get over their own childhood hurts. "In our work with sleep disturbed toddlers, we found that all their mothers were insecurely attached to their own mothers. Their non-authoritative behavior vis-à-vis their children therefore was often an attempt to make up for the harshness and insensitivity they had experienced during their own childhood. What they did not realize was the degree to which their failure to set limits reflected their own insensitivity to their children's needs...."

So not controlling your child's sleep shows insensitivity to her needs, says Minde. This *is* an interesting piece of counterintuitive information.

In Minde's work we are faced with an aspect of the parent-expert dynamic that is often present, though rarely so overtly. When experts are dismissive of parents or talk down to them, we tend to think it's because parents fall outside of the medical elite. But Minde gives us reason to suspect that this dismissiveness occurs also because the parents they advise are, overwhelmingly, female.

Admittedly, this phenomenon is based on gender roles that have been overturned: Women can be doctors, and men can be advice-seeking parents. And yet, the tradition played out by Dr. Olsen and my mother-in-law is still a part of our culture. It's in my pediatrician's patronizing "There there, a little crying won't hurt your baby" attitude, it's in Ferber's quiet insistence that breastfeeding (an exclusively female parenting experience) interferes with the development of good sleep habits, and it's in Minde's writing, where it practically jumps off the page and smacks you across the face.

What the Experts Don't Know

Joyce Barrett says, "Doctors are used to being the expert, they are used to giving advice, they are used to the idea that they know more than you do. This attitude may be appropriate with the child who has bacterial meningitis, but not many children do."

The point of all of this is not to slam doctors and sleep experts. When kids do get bacterial meningitis, or strep throat or plain old flu, parents are lucky to have doctors to help them. And if a tidal wave of truly serious sleep problems floods a family, its members will be grateful to the sleep specialist who can bail them out. But the rest of the time we need to keep expert advice in perspective. The pediatrician who tells you you need to let your baby cry at night, the sleep clinician who advocates a special program with a timer and a chart and, yes, the sleep researcher who promotes the benefits of co-sleeping—these professionals know something about kids and sleep, but they don't know the whole story. Not the way you do.

After all, you're the one who observes your child day in and day out. You know that the bunny pajamas seem to make the transition to bedtime smoother, and that she likes to fall asleep with your palm pressed to her belly. No sleep expert has your intimate sense of the quirks and characteristics that make your little one different from every other child on the planet. Better than anyone else, you understand her temperament. And although experts rarely acknowledge it, this understanding is crucial: temperament significantly affects kids' sleep habits. In the next chapter, we'll see how.

5 Temperament

THE MISSING LINK

Picture this: a maternity ward in the days before babies started rooming with their moms. A dozen newborns are tucked into individual bassinets on the other side of the nursery window. One has olive skin and a sprinkling of brown curls. Another is very fair, with a shock of black hair. There is a pair of exquisitely vulnerable baldies, one tiny, the other a hefty nine-pounder. A baby girl with a fringe of dark eyelashes has wisps of hair so pale they look almost white.

Like creatures from another planet, these brand-new beings are trying to adjust to the strange world in which they now find themselves. They do this in individual ways. A handful doze, a few bleat plaintively, one or two scream so hard that their faces become scrunched and crimson. Still others lie calmly in their plastic bassinets, eyes wide open.

I got this initial glimpse at the spectrum of babyhood as a 17-year-old aunt. Until then, I had thought that all babies were pretty much the same. But during this first encounter with my niece, Serena, and her hospital cronies, I began to realize something that's obvious to seasoned parents: No two babies are quite alike. They look different, sure, but the contrasts are not just skin-deep. Why does one baby sleep through his neighbor's loud protests while another can't help but join in? How come some infants don't mind waiting a few extra minutes for a feeding, while others anticipate each meal anxiously?

The clear differences in the way that children—even babies—respond to the world around them reflect their temperament. Often described as a child's basic disposition, temperament is something each of us is born with, and tends to persist through life. Though temperament is a complex interweaving of characteristics, researchers have identified nine separate traits that can actually be assessed from a child's earliest days. They are:

Intensity: the strength of our emotional reactions. When your child is upset, does she shed a couple of silent tears, or sob uncontrollably? Is her laugh a gentle giggle or a whole-belly roar?

Persistence: our refusal (or willingness) to take "no" for an answer. Kids who are easily redirected from one activity to another are not very persistent, while those who "lock in" and resist distraction fall at the other end of the scale.

Sensitivity: the degree to which we are aware and influenced by noises, temperatures, textures and tastes as well as emotions. A very sensitive little one might be bothered by a scratchy T-shirt label that a not-so-sensitive child wouldn't notice. She will also be influenced by *your* feelings—from stress to bliss—far more than the average child.

Perceptiveness: the extent to which we notice what goes on around us. A perceptive child will observe colors, noises and objects that others miss. He is also likely to be the one who forgets that he went upstairs to brush his teeth as soon as he lays eyes on yesterday's K'nex project.

Adaptability: the way that we cope with changes to our schedule. Children who are very adaptable can be put down for a nap when you're away on vacation as easily as they can be at home. Kids who are slow to adapt tend to be very upset by these kinds of changes in their routines. Surprises put them off, too.

Regularity: our bodies' basic rhythm. If your baby eats, eliminates and sleeps at roughly the same time every day, she's very regular. If, however, she's one of the babies who is next to impossible to schedule because every day brings a different pattern, she falls at the other end of the regularity spectrum.

Energy: our activity level. A child with high energy tends to use his whole body when he plays, and even when he sleeps. Less active kids are more likely to stay still while they sleep and engage in more quiet, seated play.

First reaction: the likelihood of our jumping in to a new activity, or holding back before participating. Some children won't hesitate in a new situation and are comfortable learning by doing. Others are a bit put off by unfamiliarity, and will learn by watching until they gain a certain level of comfort.

Mood: the trait that makes some of us "naturally cheerful," and others more serious or analytical. Kids, too, will be generally sunny and positive, or sober or grumpy—even as babies.

To Each His Own

Alexander Thomas and Stella Chess are the husband-and-wife research team who first identified these traits and showed how they can affect the parent-child relationship. In the 1950s, they conducted the now famous New York Longitudinal Study, watching 133 children dress, eat and play with friends. They also interviewed the children's parents and teachers. Their findings continue to provide the blueprint for the way we think of temperament today. In one paper, Chess wrote: "Right from the start babies are different. Each has his or her way of showing feelings and responding to the world. . . . Being alert to these temperamental differences and understanding how they require different caregiving approaches are crucial to nurturing children's healthy emotional growth."

In their research, Chess and Thomas also discovered that the nine traits cluster together in some kids, creating three temperamental types: easy kids, those who are "slow to warm up" and "high-need" (a.k.a.

"difficult") children. (See the "Snapshot" boxes, below and on the following pages, for more on these types.) The purpose of delineating these categories is not simply to stick kids with labels; that, any parent of a willful child will tell you, can be counterproductive. Rather, as Chess

---

SNAPSHOT OF AN EASY BABY

As an infant, Daniel was unusually calm and serene. When he was hungry or lonely, he'd fuss a bit and eventually cry for attention, but otherwise he was pretty quiet. He almost never worked himself into a real lather throughout the early months the way his older brother did. Putting him to sleep was a breeze—he'd either fall asleep at the breast or just nod off in the car, the stroller, or even in his chair in the family room. At around 6 months, he became more aware of and interested in the things and people around him, so his parents started to take a bit more care when putting him down for the night. They'd take him into his darkened room, sing him a song or read him a short story and then lay him in his crib. He cried for—no kidding—six minutes on the first night. And that was it.

---

explains, recognizing your child's temperament is an important step in understanding who he is and supporting his development.

Not every child will fall into one of these groups—many kids' traits don't arrange themselves in any particular pattern. But extremes in even one or two of the nine categories—intensity or persistence, for example—can have a big impact on behavior. And although sleep experts rarely acknowledge it, that means behavior at night as well as during the day.

Parents who have more than one child often figure this out for themselves. As one mom, Lee Ouellette, says, "My daughter, who is now 3½, has horrible sleep habits. From the time she was 6 weeks old she refused to take a nap during the day and I knew that her sleep was important and that she slept better with me than by herself. I didn't think it was a big deal at the time. Thirteen months later her brother arrived. Now here's a boy who *loves* his sleep. Two naps a day until he was two and a full 11–12 hours every night. Every mother's dream child, especially after the Energizer baby."

Reading Lee's story, it's tempting to chalk her daughter's restlessness up to inexperienced parenting. You may say, "She was a new mom, she didn't set up a routine, and that's why her daughter didn't sleep well. When she had her second child, she knew what she was doing, and that's how he became a good sleeper." And a parent's actions and atti-

---

SNAPSHOT OF A SLOW-TO-WARM-UP BABY

Marcy is often affectionate and good tempered. As a baby, she'd crawl and later cruise around her home happily. But if something unexpected happened—like a neighbor dropping over to say hello—Marcy would become clingy and withdrawn, often hiding her face in her mother's hair for the entire visit. Now a toddler, Marcy has attended several music classes at the library. But she has not yet ventured from her mom's lap to participate in the singing and dancing.

Marcy also has more than the usual difficulty with transitions. Knowing this, her parents take special care to make sure her bedtime routine is unhurried and reassuring; the predictable steps help Marcy feel more in control and ease her towards lights-out. As their daughter matures, Marcy's mom and dad are finding new ways to deal with her tentative nature. They try to tell her about their plans and what is going to happen next, and that advance notice seems to make a big difference.

---

tudes *can* make a difference in children's sleep habits—but less often than you might think.

Tracy MacDonald is just one of many moms whose *second* child turned out to be the wakeful one: "When my daughter started eating cereal at 4 months we decided that it was time to teach her to sleep on her own. The first time I let her cry it was 17 minutes and I was in the kitchen holding the counter watching the clock saying to myself 'I can't go in, I can't go in.' She made it through and is now a great sleeper. I am sure you could dance a jig on her bed and she wouldn't even roll over.

"Her brother, my second, took a little longer and is not as sound a sleeper as she is. This, I think, is because he is more needy than she is. Every time I open his door to look in on him he stirs. He likes every minute he can get with Mommy. I used the same method and he was close to 7 months when he fell asleep on his own."

Or maybe it's the third child who's the most challenging at night. Jean Barry says, "I didn't do anything different with my children but they all have different sleep habits. My first slept through at 5 weeks, my second child slept through at 10 weeks and my youngest is 17 months and still wakes up between three and five times in the night."

Temperament and the Sleep Experts

In spite of its commonsense appeal and the solid research behind it, the notion of temperament and the role it plays in parenting hasn't made a dent in the sleep experts' books.

You can't even find the word "temperament" in the index of Ferber's *Solve Your Child's Sleep Problems*. Instead, you find this:

If your child is a restless sleeper or can't seem to settle down at night, you should be very cautious about assuming that he is just a poor sleeper or doesn't need as much sleep as other children of the same age. Your own expectations can have a very strong influence on how your child's sleep patterns develop from the day you bring him home from the hospital. I have seen many families who were told by the nurses in the maternity ward, 'Your baby hardly sleeps at all. You're in for trouble!' Because these parents were led to believe their child was just a poor sleeper and there wasn't anything they could do about it, they allowed their baby to develop poor sleep habits.

Although Ferber's maternity-ward nurses clearly recognize that babies are different from day one, the sleep specialist dismisses these observations, making it seem as if sleep habits are 100 percent nurture and zero percent nature.

If your kids are relatively easygoing and adaptable, this possibility may not be so farfetched. Tricia Maxwell is a mom who finds that nighttime *can* be pretty restful. "For me, night waking has not been a major problem. I think it is because I instill a bedtime routine very early in my children's lives. With my 4-year-old I started a bedtime routine around 3 months. With my 2-year-old I started a bedtime routine almost from birth. My bedtime routine consists of bathtime, story and cuddle time and a song. After that, lights out. The only time they wake in the night is when they are sick or have a nightmare. I guess I am lucky."

Sleep expert and author Marc Weissbluth would approve of Maxwell's bedtime routine, but he would likely say that luck had nothing to do with her success. His book *Healthy Sleep Habits, Happy Child* is oddly inconsistent that way: Although he devotes a couple of pages to an explanation of temperament and Chess and Thomas's research (though he mentions only Thomas), the rest of his book almost completely ignores the you-have-to-work-with-what-you-get facet of parenting.

Take, for example, his trademark claim that an early bedtime (between 6 and 8 p.m. and the earlier the better) will make your child "more charming, more sweet." What happens if she was never sweet to begin with? Exhaustion can certainly darken a sunny disposition, but no amount of rest will turn a feisty-natured child into a docile one. Similarly, he writes, "You should not assume that it is natural for all children to get peevish, irritable or cranky at the end of the day. Well-rested children do not behave this way." Who are these well-rested wonders? You have only to visit the mall to find children behaving peevishly not just at the end of the day, but at the beginning and the middle, too. I guess *some* of them might be tired *some* of the time. But others are simply slow to warm up, or prone to moodiness or over-stimulated by the lights and noise of the mall.

How can Weissbluth know that your child will be ready for bed before 8 p.m. anyway? What if she's naturally a late-to-rise-late-to-sleep kind of person, just like her mom or dad? Or maybe she simply doesn't need so much sleep. Weissbluth dismisses point-blank this latter possibility and the havoc it might create through ungodly-hour wake-ups:

SLEEP SURVEY STATS

When we asked, "Why do babies sleep through the night at such different ages?"

- **64% of respondents agreed (either "strongly" or "somewhat") with the statement: "Babies sleep through the night at different ages because of differences in how parents handle bedtime and night waking."**
- **Even more—96%—agreed that "Babies sleep through the night at different ages because of differences in temperament and individual development."**

"[One of] the most common inhibiting fears in putting your child to bed early [is] that he will start the day too early..." But, he says, "your child will not get up earlier and earlier because of an early bedtime." He backs up his claim with vague "sleep begets sleep" logic, implying that all parents have to do is exercise the right control (become your child's "timekeeper," he urges) in order to get their kids to sleep long and deep. It sounds good, but is it real life?

Weissbluth and Ferber are not the only ones whose methods fail to integrate temperamental considerations.

Popular discipline guides tend to focus on matching the consequence of misbehavior to the "crime": if a child is acting antisocial, use time-out; if she is misusing a toy, remove the toy. But rarely are parents encouraged to also match their responses to their child's temperament: Should the sensitive kid who bursts into tears after a firm reminder to share be dealt with in the same way as a persistent child who continues to pull toys out of others' hands after repeated reprimands? Similarly, can the intense child who startles awake with his heart pounding be expected to return to sleep as easily as the child who surfaces gently and peacefully?

How Knowing Your Child Can Help

Mary Sheedy Kurcinka, author of *Raising Your Spirited Child* and *Kids, Parents and Power Struggles*, is one expert who does take temperament concerns seriously. Her books are filled with realistic portrayals of life with harder-to-parent children, and solid yet flexible advice to help their families cope.

In her chapter "Bedtime and Night Waking" in *Raising Your Spirited Child*, Sheedy Kurcinka talks about understanding the role your child plays in alleviating nighttime struggles: "Is she sensitive and easily over stimulated? Is she persistent and hates to take a break? Is she irregular, needs little sleep and doesn't fall into a schedule? Are transitions difficult for her—is making the move to bedtime stressful? Is she active and always on the move? Are her protests powerful because she is intense? Each of these traits makes relaxing and falling asleep more difficult to accomplish."

But it's not just a matter of passive understanding. There are a number of proactive steps parents can take to help their kids cope better at night. Naturally, the approach that's right for your child will be dictated by your child's temperament.

Let's look at some examples:

The intense child has strong reactions. That includes the transition to bedtime as well as the experience of waking in the night. That's why he probably needs help to relax and stay calm until he starts to drift. "There are hoards of books on sleep problems that will encourage you to let your child cry it out," says Sheedy Kurcinka. "There is a flaw in this advice. Supposedly the child stops crying after a few minutes. Spirited kids don't. Left to their own devices, intense, spirited children become overwhelmed by their powerful reactions. They may be unable to stop, crying for hours instead of minutes. They get more upset as the minutes tick away. The bedtime battle is extended instead of shortened."

Finding yourself in this boat with a baby is not easy. But it won't be long before you spot dry land. When your child reaches toddlerhood, for example, Sheedy Kurcinka says, "you might try pulling a chair into his room and reading the newspaper, folding the laundry, or reading a good book until he falls asleep." And preschoolers "are old enough to keep the image of you with them even though you are separate. That's why we can expect them to begin staying in their room."

The sensitive child needs to go to sleep in comfort. Those one-piece pajamas with feet and bits of lace might be sweet, but the seams across the toes and the scratchy fabric at the neck may very well drive your sensitive little one nuts. And because sensitive children are easily over-stimulated, you might have to work a bit harder at controlling the nighttime environment in your home. Turn off the telephone ringers and keep older children out of earshot, or artificially darken your child's bedroom with cardboard behind the drapes if noise and light seem to be disruptive.

Sensitive children also need to feel *emotionally* comfortable in order to sleep peacefully. Once again, for babies, this may mean nothing less than your physical presence, but reassuring words and a soothing routine will work for some toddlers and almost all preschoolers. Because sensitive children are prone to worrying, Sheedy Kurcinka recommends statements that will normalize what they are feeling. For example: "It's all right to lie here quietly. You will fall asleep soon. You are not sick." Or "You don't need a lot of sleep but it's time for Mom and Dad to have some time alone so you have to stay in your room."

The persistent child pushes the boundaries at every turn. Most young kids are easy to distract, but it can be next to impossible to divert a temperamentally persistent child of even 13 or 14 months once he sets his mind to something.

SNAPSHOT OF A HIGH-NEED BABY

Almost from the day she was born, Kate has been demanding by day and restless by night. It seems to her mother that she did not get properly dressed more than a few times during Kate's infancy, because so often she was positioned with her shirt pulled up and her needy baby at her breast.

Unlike the children who squeal and giggle at playgroup, Kate is upset by tiny things: a loud truck honking, a long ride in the car, the "wrong" kind of juice. And once she starts wailing, getting her to stop isn't easy. "Why is she like this? Is it our fault?" her parents used to ask each other.

But when Kate entered her second year and showed no signs of changing, her mom and dad learned that there are other babies like their own little fireball, and that the characteristics that make her tougher to parent come as naturally to her as her copper hair and sparkly eyes. So instead of trying to fight her temperament and mold her into the "perfect" child, *they* have started to adapt. They bought a dozen pairs of socks like the ones she always wants to wear and have put the pairs with the big thick seams in a box in the basement. They have also packed away the sleep training manuals they borrowed and have developed their own somewhat complicated but wholly workable nighttime routine. Although others often frown on these "accommodations," Kate's parents know that they prevent stressful meltdowns and make their family life better.

Parents dealing with persistence need to anticipate problems and make their limits very clear. Says Sheedy Kurcinka, "If you read books during your bedtime ritual, decide before you start how many you are willing to read, who picks them out, and how long they can be. If you have a snack, clarify what foods are appropriate for the bedtime snack and which ones are not before making a choice. Once you set bedtime, use a timer or clock to prove that it is bedtime." Similarly, if you decide that your persistent child can join you in bed upon her first night waking, but not at bedtime, tell her over and over that that's the way it's going to be, and stick to your guns.

On the other hand, the expression "pick your battles" was probably coined for these kids. Since you don't want to be fighting with them all the time, decide what really matters, and let the rest go. "Be clear about what bedtime means," Sheedy Kurcinka says. "Does it mean in bed? If so, whose bed, yours or mine? Does it mean anywhere in the bedroom? Is falling asleep on the floor acceptable?"

The energetic child probably gets hyper at bedtime. It may look like he needs to play, but you won't mellow him out with an evening wrestling match or a trip to the park. Rather, his energy will just build and build until he explodes in a tantrum or a torrent of tears.

Babies with this trait are often restless once they're in bed, too. They keep themselves awake at night rocking back and forth when they're desperate to crawl, or they pull themselves up on the crib rail even though they can't get down without falling. Although sleep training experts like Weissbluth say that parents shouldn't hang around to help these little dynamos lie down and relax and that there's nothing wrong with the alternative, some parents may not be keen on leaving a child until he's so wiped that he falls asleep standing up!

Energetic children need lots of running and jumping and climbing during the day, but not at night. After dark, they benefit from a soothing bath, calming stories and other gentle activities to help them wind down.

The high-need child has a number of "difficult" traits clustered together, making the first year or two particularly challenging for both her and her parents. High-need babies—

- **have a low sensory threshold.** Anything from a sleeper tag to an older child's loud voice can set them off.
- **are unable to self-soothe.** These little ones need parental intervention—carrying, rocking, singing—to settle when other babies might just nod off.
- **are light sleepers.** They tend to be easily wakened and have difficulty falling back to sleep.
- **are alert and easily distracted.** For example, many high-need babies can't nurse in a room with the TV on—it's just too interesting.
- **need lots of sucking.** Most want to nurse frequently, or will suck bottle nipples, as well as pacifiers, thumbs and fingers for comfort.
- **are irregular.** They often sleep, feed and poop at different times each day.

According to William Sears, renowned pediatrician and author of *The Fussy Baby*, we should try to look at these traits in a positive light. "A baby who fusses when put to sleep alone, or fusses if no one picks him up, has the strength of character to assert his personality and tell his caregiver what he needs." And, says Sears, meeting these needs, and developing a parenting style that suits them as well as the rest of the family, will bring out the best in that child.

High-Need Baby Survival Guide

So you know that your baby really *is* different, that it's not your fault and that all that nursing, carrying, comforting and entertaining will pay off one day. Nevertheless, you are probably cranky, unshowered and exhausted. How can you cope?

- **Don't worry about spoiling**—especially if your baby is under 6 months. Research shows that the faster we respond to a crying infant, the more easily she will be soothed. Studies also prove that babies who are treated responsively learn to use more non-crying forms of communication by the age of 1 year. So go ahead and rock your baby to sleep or bring him into bed if that works for you. Surviving and getting a little rest is what's important right now. You'll have plenty of time for formal limit-setting later on.

- **Get carried away.** Baby carriers don't only free up your hands, they also give your little one a ride that is almost as close and comforting as the one she enjoyed in the womb. Many parents of high-need babies find that their kids drift into sleep more easily in a carrier, too. That means they offer an easier route to naps *and* a way to prevent the kind of overtiredness that makes nighttime sleep more challenging.
- **Unplug.** When it's time for your baby's nap, unplug the phones, tape over the doorbell, let the outside world and your role in it slide for an hour or two if you possibly can. Some parents of high-need children claim their daily siestas absolutely saved them during the first year. I even know of a working mom who locked her door and napped in her office over lunch hour until her child reached toddlerhood.
- **Don't be a hero.** Being a good parent does not mean doing everything yourself. So when your partner offers to take the night shift, or your mother says she'll come over early so that you can go back to bed, say "OK, thanks," not "I can manage." And if the offers aren't forthcoming, don't be afraid to ask for help. You'll find a way to repay the favor once your life becomes a little easier.

Where Do I Fit In?

With all of this careful consideration of your child and her traits, it's easy to miss one other important aspect of temperament: your own.

Your own nature can make a major difference in how you feel about bedtime and night waking. Maybe you find sleep training fairly easy, not only because your child is easygoing but because you yourself are adaptable and slow to become upset. On the other hand, perhaps letting your baby cry means a sleepless night for you even after your baby has conked out, because your own intensity and sensitivity leave you anxious and wired.

Either way, your temperament, in combination with your child's, is going to shape your parenting style and your family life, by day and by night. Taking stock of who your child is and working with that profile isn't indulgent—it's smart and constructive. Similarly, factoring in your own and your partner's gut response to night waking isn't copping out (or wimping out)—it's being practical. The goal, after all, is not to master the sleep-training method or the family-bed arrangement that works for others. It's to figure out what works for you.

6 The Generation Gap

WHY OUR PARENTS DON'T UNDERSTAND

Sophie is close to her mother. Nevertheless, she doesn't talk to her about Jack's sleep habits. She has a handful of friends with babies around the same age as her 10-month-old, and when they get together for oversized mugs of French roast, the four women speak of little else. None of their children sleep through the night consistently, so they can easily relate to Sophie's weariness.

But Sophie's mother can't. She tries to be sympathetic to her daughter's plight; still, she just doesn't understand why her grandson wakes up at night. In her day, it was simple: After the newborn stage, you put the baby down in the evening, and you got him out of his crib in the morning. Period. Sophie has heard all this before and doesn't really want to hear it again—it makes her feel sort of incompetent—and that's why she steers clear of sleep talk with her mom.

Sophie's mother-in-law is several years younger than her mom, and her parenting style is quite different from the one Sophie was raised with. Nevertheless, little Jack's other grandma also has trouble accepting his night waking. She's not so much critical as incredulous. "What do you *mean* the baby still doesn't sleep through the night? How can that be?"

Do you recognize a little of yourself in Sophie? Or maybe it's your friend, sister or co-worker whom she reminds you of. Perhaps you thought this kind of uneasy mother-daughter dynamic could be chalked up to personality clashes or latent rebellious tendencies. Well, guess what? The gap between Sophie and her mother(s) is more generational than individual: Our sleep survey shows that night waking is a touchy topic for many young parents and their parents. Why are so many of today's grandparents honestly unable to relate to their adult children's night life? The answer lies in the way that parenting practices have changed over the past 30 years, while attitudes toward sleep have remained stuck in the past.

The Times, They Are...Uh...Changing?

If you want to look at a crystal clear example of evolving parenting ideals, consider the notion of spoiling. Our mothers (and to a lesser extent, our fathers—that's another difference) were cautioned against raising spoiled kids. So great was the concern that even tiny babies were treated with careful restraint. In a 1960s edition of *Baby and Child Care*, Benjamin Spock explains it this way: "If a mother is too ready to pick a baby up and carry him around whenever he fusses, she may find after a couple of months that he is fretting and holding out his arms to be carried almost all the time when he is awake. If she continues to give in, he realizes after a while that he has his poor tired mother under his thumb and he becomes increasingly disagreeable and tyrannical in demanding this service." And Spock was considered one of the more permissive experts of his time!

If you were a 1960s housewife who had her act together, you got that little one "on a schedule" as soon as possible. You controlled feedings and made sure they occurred around four hours apart. You also left your baby in her crib or playpen periodically during the day, whether she was awake or asleep, so that she would learn to "entertain herself." If you didn't do these things, you might just find yourself reading Spock's advice on how to "unspoil":

Make out a schedule for yourself, on paper if necessary, that requires you to be busy with housework or anything else for most of the time the baby is awake. Go at it with a great bustle—to impress the baby and to impress yourself. When he frets and raises his arms, explain to him in a friendly but very firm tone that this job and that job *must* get done this afternoon.

Today, parents' priorities have shifted a bit. Worries about spoiling are still around, but they have been trumped by a new focus on responsive parenting. A baby's first crucial "emotional lesson," we are told, is to develop trust and form a strong attachment to her caregivers. Experts like Penelope Leach explain that your loving attention is key not just to your child's short-term happiness, but to her overall well-being. In *Your Baby and Child*, Leach writes, "If your baby is ever to be a communicative, competent, confident person, it's important that she...learns that you come when she cries." As far as concerns about spoiling go, Leach says "there's no such thing as too much attention and comforting,

WORKING IT OUT

Working outside the home is about twice as common today as it was when most of our mothers were raising us. This, too, has an impact on night waking and the way we post-millennial parents look at it. However, it's hard to say whether working outside the home makes mothers more or less motivated to get their kids sleeping through the night—a paying job can pull in either direction, or both at once.

On one hand, many contemporary moms who have a terrible time with night waking during their maternity leave cope by napping or keeping irregular hours. But once back at work, siestas and early bedtimes are hard to manage, and these women realize that they absolutely cannot function unless they find a way to get their child to sleep more at night.

At the same time, most moms working at jobs feel they need to make the most of the time they have with their kids. These women may be more likely to consider the nighttime relationship—whether it involves rocking or breastfeeding or co-sleeping—an important way to add some of the unhurried together time that they feel they miss during the day. Nor are dads immune. Husband-and-wife surgeons I once knew worked long, intense hours at the hospital during the day and then positively relished bringing their kids into their bed at night for cuddles and closeness. In cases like this, night waking may go on through the first year and into the second, but it is considered a reasonable trade-off.

play, talk and laughter, too many smiles and hugs, even too many presents and treats, as long as parents, or whoever is in charge, give them because they want to...."

Recent public education campaigns promoting the importance of early brain development take all of this a step further. Invest in Kids, one of several organizations devoted to raising parents' consciousness, ran a series of TV and transit ads in 1999/2000 depicting one young child dressed as an eggplant, and another as a flower. The copy said: "Will a child lie and vegetate, or blossom intellectually?"

The veggie metaphor is a bit much, and it has the unfortunate power of putting some already attentive parents in a panic when they hire a sitter for a mere evening out. But many moms and dads accept the overall message and eagerly give their children as much responsive care as possible. They eschew their mothers' playpens in favor of baby carriers; they order Chinese food instead of trying to juggle a clingy child and a frying pan; they let the laundry pile up so that they can connect during half an hour of peek-a-boo before bedtime.

But when they turn off the lights, they are also expected to turn off this style of parenting. By telling parents to ignore their babies' cries, or to respond when the clock—and not the child—says it's time, the sleep experts tell people *not* to do the very things that have come to define them as good parents during the day. It's a difficult emotional shift for many parents, and it's probably no easier for their children. After all, many of our babies have been led to expect that when they call, someone will come.

So maybe it really *was* simpler for moms like Sophie's. Letting their babies cry a little at night didn't represent a huge departure from what they did during the day. As a result, they didn't have to feel so conflicted about it. And their babies probably did cry less than some of ours do, because being left alone now and then was part of their daytime reality, too. So, yeah, mom, you were right. Giving babies "too much" attention probably does make them more demanding. But it also builds their brains and makes them feel secure.

In contrast, today's Hot and Cold Guide to Parenting can make us feel as though our hearts will split in two. By day we are encouraged to crawl inside our child's head and feel what he feels. At night, however, we are not supposed to empathize. Rather, we should, as one sleep guru says, learn to tell the difference between a "sad cry" and "a cry of protest." We seem to be caught in a cultural transition that hasn't quite worked itself out.

The extent of the contradiction struck me all at once when Leo and I went out of town to visit a childhood friend of mine. At around 8 p.m., my friend led 6-month-old Leo and me to an out-of-the-way bedroom in the rambling country house where we were staying. Her mother followed us upstairs and proudly pulled a baby monitor she had been saving for just such an occasion out of its box. After I had sung Leo to sleep, we turned on the monitor and headed back to the living room to watch *High Fidelity*. I don't know if it was because of the traveling or the strange bed or some other factor, but less than an hour later, Leo was awake and calling loudly through the monitor. As I headed upstairs to re-settle him, I heard my friend's mother say, "Maybe these things aren't such a good idea after all." And what she said made a kind of sense. Why amplify your child's every arousal and crib-bound protest if you're supposed to turn a deaf ear in order to teach independent sleep? Using baby monitors in a sleep culture stuck circa 1960 is as anachronistic as the telephones on *The Flintstones*.

Of course this duality isn't problematic for everyone. Some parents may simply have two modes: Day is the time for cuddles and closeness and quick responses, night is the time to sleep *sans* mama and papa. Babies handled this way, will, eventually, adapt. For those with easy-going temperaments, the adjustment will probably be pretty painless. But as we saw in Chapter Five, babies with more intense temperaments can have a difficult go of it.

Ready, Steady...

Worrying more about stimulation than spoiling is just one way that we parent differently from our own parents. Another change involves our take on developmental milestones. A generation ago, moms and dads really kept on top of these; in fact, they pushed them along. Dr. Olsen, my mother-in-law's pediatrician, published a booklet recommending introducing solid food as early as three or four weeks of age, for instance. The concept of a child's readiness, today an important consideration, was not often talked about. If a parent (or, perhaps more likely, her doctor) decided it was time to start cereal, it didn't matter if the baby's "extrusion reflex" made her push food out faster than mom could spoon it in, or if she was still too tiny to sit up.

Today we introduce solids differently, recognizing that a natural window opens if you wait a little bit. Part of this is based on science: We know that babies under 4 months are biologically immature—the enzymes, kidneys, intestinal membrane and immune system are not yet fully developed. This makes it hard for them to digest solid food. It also makes them more vulnerable to food allergies.

Equally important is the emphasis we now place on individual development: Has the baby stopped pushing everything but milk out with her tongue? Can she sit upright, with a little help, perhaps? Has she reached the stage of "putting everything in her mouth"? No chart or doctor can anticipate exactly when all this will happen, so solids are recommended between 4 and 6 months. At this age, food isn't something you're doing *to* your child; she is ready to be an active participant in the feeding process. That's the idea. In fact, some experts suggest that parents let their *babies* decide exactly when it's time for solids. Pediatrician Jack Newman (and co-author Teresa Pitman) describe it this way in *Dr. Jack Newman's Guide to Breastfeeding*: At around 4 months, "the baby will become very interested in the eating process. He will follow the food on the fork from your plate to your mouth, and there is no doubt that this is fascinating for him. By 5 or 6 months, many babies will try to grab that food, and try to put it into their mouths. They're ready to eat, aren't they?"

Although some of today's young parents are quite comfortable relying on baby's signals, this approach represents a child-centeredness that would have been unthinkable a generation ago. I can hear it now: "Letting the *baby* decide when it's time for solid food? Who's ever heard of anything so ridiculous? What does a baby know?"

Toilet training conventions have undergone a similar transformation. Everyone knows someone who brags about having trained their child at 11 or 12 months. My 1960s Spock is a bit more progressive. In it the doctor writes, "Early in the second year...the child gets the idea of giving presents and takes lots of satisfaction from this...This joy in giving plays a part in his willingness to give up his movement at his mother's request....It's also at about a year that a baby becomes fascinated with putting things in containers....These general aspects of readiness give a mother some basis for starting training at this age if she wishes to."

But we now recognize that most children can't begin to take notice of their need to "go" nor to manage the mechanics of pulling their pants up and down until about a year later. It's another big step from noticing how these bodily functions work to controlling them—a step that takes anywhere from a few more months to well over a year. So although it's possible to plunk a very regular 1-year-old on the potty in time to catch his pee and poop, most experts and parents realize that the process works better when kids are able to take an active role.

Learning to sleep through the night represents a developmental process, too. But once again, the thinking in the sleep arena more closely resembles the last generation's parenting views than our own. It's not that experts don't see sleeping through the night as a milestone. They most certainly do. In his 1992 book, *Touchpoints*, T. Berry Brazelton writes: "I am convinced that while a child's independence may not be easy for parents to accept, it is an exciting and rewarding goal for the child. Being able to manage alone at night helps a child develop a positive self-image and gives her a real feeling of strength."

Perhaps what's difficult for some parents to accept is not a child's independence at night, but the age and stage at which this is supposed to arrive. Maybe sleeping through the night is similar to eating solid food and toilet training—sure, you can make it happen early, but it's likely to be much less of a struggle if you wait a little while. After all, does it make sense to talk about "a rewarding goal" and "a positive self-image" in relation to an infant? What cues does a young baby give us to tell us he's ready and eager to sleep independently? Not the same kind of cues as he gives when he leans open-mouthed towards a spoonful of rice cereal or strains to crawl toward a toy, that's for sure.

"My son just turned 20 months yesterday and for the past two nights, he has slept all the way through without waking, all on his own, with no training required. I believe he needed the nighttime comforting and nursing and is coming to an age and place developmentally where he doesn't need them and he's secure enough to let go on his own."
—*Rhonda Ploubis*

The Breastfeeding Difference

There's another major difference in parenting since our moms had babies: We have changed from a bottle-feeding culture to a breastfeeding culture. In my mother's milieu, breastfeeding was just not done. Her doctor didn't encourage it, and her friends dismissed it as primitive. To mom and her peers, formula was more sophisticated, more advanced. "Why ruin your breasts and chain yourself to your baby when there is a much tidier alternative?" they thought. Reflected even in the word "formula" is the postwar infatuation with stuff manufactured by a lab instead of by nature.

These days we recognize formula as a reasonable feeding alternative, but it's breast milk that is promoted as the perfect food for infants. Doctors and nurses, friends and even strangers are more likely to encourage nursing mothers than they are to scorn them. According to a survey by The Canadian Institute of Child Health, 74 percent of Canadian women (over 80 percent in several provinces) breastfed their newborns in 1993. A similar number—75 percent—of the *Today's Parent* Sleep Survey respondents said they nursed their babies. While the U.S. figure is lower—about 60 percent in 1995—the majority of new babies are breastfed and the American Academy of Pediatrics is enthusiastically promoting breastfeeding.

Not only does this supportive climate mean that more women breastfeed, it also means they nurse more openly, more flexibly and for longer. One courageous woman, now in her 60s, who ignored her family's disdain in order to breastfeed her children, told me that she wouldn't have dreamed of leaving the house if it meant she might have to nurse in public. My local Starbucks, meanwhile, is frequented by businesspeople and singles as well as mothers. It sports a pink sticker in the window that says "You are welcome to breastfeed here."

Nursing mothers feed more often, too. A four-hour feeding schedule was the norm for a generation of bottle-fed babies. But breast milk digests more easily and therefore more quickly than formula, so feedings are scheduled much closer together, if they are scheduled at all. More often, and at the advice of breastfeeding professionals, babies are simply nursed "on demand." In fact, many breastfeeding experts advise parents to respond to their babies' hunger cues, such as sucking fists or rooting, without waiting for them to demand at all. As a 1997 American Academy of Pediatrics statement suggests, "Crying is a *late* indicator of hunger."

In spite of this seismic shift in the way many parents nourish their little ones, data collected on bottle-fed babies continue to shape how sleep experts define normal infant sleep-wake patterns, says sleep researcher James McKenna. "That so many more mothers are now breastfeeding their infants for increasingly longer periods makes sleep models based only on data from infants fed artificial or cow's milk (from bottles) highly problematic for at least half of the population of contemporary American infants."

Why? What does feeding have to do with sleep, anyway?

Quite a lot, as it turns out. "Bottle-fed infants exhibit significantly different nightly sleep profiles than do breastfed infants," McKenna reports. Specifically, bottle feeding leads to an increase in quiet sleep whereas breastfeeding leads babies to sleep more lightly and wake more often as they move from stage to stage.

Co-sleeping is another factor that comes into play with breastfeeding, and it doesn't apply just to family bed devotees: Any mom who has had to get up every hour or two to nurse knows the practical benefits of spending a few nights sleeping with baby in bed, on a futon or even in a rocking chair.

As we saw in Chapter Three, sleeping close to you further alters your baby's sleep patterns. It also puts even more distance between our generation and the one before us. "Infant sleep studies were first conducted by researchers in the fifties and sixties when breastfeeding was at an all-time low and co-sleeping was regarded as being aberrant, and definitely to be avoided," writes McKenna. "Since the significance of mother-infant co-sleeping with nighttime breastfeeding was considered neither biologically nor culturally appropriate, it is not surprising that patterns of childhood sleep development considered clinically 'healthy' and 'normal' were those patterns expressed by bottle-fed infants sleeping alone in sleep laboratories."

Breastfeeding makes a difference to the way parents *feel* at night, too. You can't measure a nursing baby's intake. So where a bottle-feeding parent might be able to think, "I just watched him drink five ounces of milk so I know he's not hungry and I'm going to wait and see if he settles," it's much harder for a breastfeeding mom to be sure. What if the baby *is* still hungry, or is hungry again? After all, there are times during the day when he feeds every hour.

The tendency to breastfeed longer plays a part, too. It is only in recent years that the American Academy of Pediatrics has upped its recommendation to suggest that women breastfeed for a year or more. In Canada, the Canadian Paediatric Society and Health Canada do not specify an ideal minimum but have given their official blessing to moms who wish to breastfeed "for up to two years of age and beyond."

"It's hard enough to withhold a bottle of juice or milk in the middle of the night. But at least you can still cuddle and comfort your baby. But when you refuse to breastfeed your baby, it's your body, your self that you're refusing."—Jane Cook

Nearly 60 percent of our own survey respondents breastfed, or planned to breastfeed, for eight months or more. Previously, many mothers who did breastfeed were likely to do so for just a few months. But, McKenna says, "Infants breastfed for a year or more develop different sleep patterns than do infants breastfed for only the first three months."

Parents who continue to breastfeed past the 3- or 4-month mark don't need a sleep researcher to tell them that. Although night waking may start with nursing babies needing more feedings, it often goes well beyond the infant being hungry in the night, because breastfeeding is also a physical relationship and does create strong associations—of comfort, of closeness, and of a certain rhythm. So contemporary young mothers can find themselves wrestling with a dilemma that is completely alien to their moms. In the days when babies were bottle-fed, or breastfed for just a short time, the night routine was not intertwined with the compelling pull of a breastfeeding relationship.

Front to Back

There is one more very concrete reason why your mom, or even your older sister, might have had her kids sleeping through the night before you even got yours down to two or three wakings: sleep positioning.

Until the last decade, doctors generally advised parents to put their infants to sleep on their stomachs. This "prone" position was believed to be best because it seemed to guard against choking. It also promoted longer periods of deeper sleep.

McKenna writes: "Since the goal of both parents and health professionals in western societies was and continues to be to promote sleep, and not awakenings, it is easy to understand why earlier data provided evidence for why infants should be placed in the prone position."

Some of the data McKenna refers to comes from research conducted in 1972. The study found that prone-sleeping newborns did sleep longer and deeper than their supine (back)-sleeping counterparts. In addition, infants who slept on their backs moved twice as much during sleep and awakened more often than babies who slept on their tummies.

Nevertheless, today we have a more vital reason to put babies to sleep on their backs. Although nobody knows exactly why, reversing the sleeping position of an infant—from front to back—has proven to be the single most important factor in reducing the chances of sudden infant death syndrome (SIDS). According to McKenna, SIDS rates have declined as much as 90 percent in some countries because of this change.

"It has been suggested that some infants who die of SIDS perhaps cannot arouse or awaken easily or fast enough to terminate a cardio-respiratory crisis during sleep, especially while in deep sleep where arousal thresholds are higher," McKenna reports. So, he notes, it may be that a child who sleeps on his back is better protected from SIDS *precisely because* he will sleep more lightly and move more often than he would if he slept on his front. And yet, most sleep experts still urge parents to get their kids sleeping with as few arousals as possible, as early as possible.

Whether the lighter sleep invited by the supine position is, in fact, the very thing that helps to ward off SIDS or not, there is no question that our practice of putting babies down this way means that they wake more easily than we did as kids.

W rap up all of these factors together—the greater emphasis on attachment and stimulation and the lesser on spoiling, the more "baby-led" approach toward developmental milestones, the proliferation of breastfeeding and the switch in sleep positions—and it becomes clear that we don't raise babies like we used to. Because so many aspects of infant care directly involve or carry over into sleep, it is absolutely natural that sleep patterns would reflect these changes. And yet, our cultural expectations have made few allowances for the developments of the past 30 years.

Holding present-day baby and child care practices up against those of other generations is one way to get a sense of just how fickle and faddish some of our assumptions and "medical" assertions about sleep and kids can be. Another way? Looking at North American parenting customs and beliefs against those of other cultures from around the world. That's what the next chapter is all about.

7 Half a World Away

DIFFERENT CULTURES, DIFFERENT SLEEP

It's the start of another workday, and the woman rises quickly to prepare herself and her infant daughter for a day on the go. But instead of changing her baby into a clean diaper, loading her into a car seat and bidding her a tearful goodbye at the daycare door, the young mother lines an animal-skin sling with soft, fresh grass. Then she drapes the *kaross* across her front and settles her tiny girl within its folds. The pair is now ready to go out and gather food, fulfilling this woman's role as a member of the !Kung San tribe of the Kalahari Desert.

Although she will spend several hours suspended near her mom's hip, the San baby is unlikely to become bored. After all, she will be soothed by the constant motion of her mom's body, entertained by the surrounding sights and sounds of the Kalahari, and kept company by her mom's co-workers, the other members of the tribe. She can also amuse herself by wriggling her arms, legs, fingers and toes, since the *kaross* is designed to hold babies loosely and to allow for lots of movement. Or like other San babies, she can touch and grab the brightly colored strands of beads her mother wears around her neck. All these diversions are important, because the semi-nomadic !Kung San don't cart around a lot of baby toys.

Not much further west and a whole lot further north, a woman in Holland checks her watch. She, too, needs to get food for her family, but she can't leave until her sister arrives to take care of her baby boy. Although the market is only a short distance from home, the 30-something mom doesn't want to take her little boy with her. Like most Dutch parents, she is committed to keeping her baby on a firm schedule, and it will soon be nap time. Besides, she holds the common Dutch belief that babies are easily overstimulated, and the supermarket—with all its loud noises and vivid hues—could simply be too much for her little son.

These two mothers have very different—in fact, nearly opposite—approaches to caring for their babies. And yet, each is doing the "right" thing. That's because our notion of the correct way to raise a child is almost entirely culture-bound. It's hard to say, absolutely, whether babies benefit more from being included in everything that goes on around them, or from protection against the sometimes frenetic hustle and bustle of adult life. Similarly, nobody really knows what's better—a regular nap or an ad-hoc approach to daytime snoozing. Most of what we "know" is based on whether these practices are favored or frowned upon in the context of our own society.

Rather than searching for absolute truth, then, it makes sense to look at the kaleidoscope of child care practices from around the world in relation to one another. When we do, we come to realize just how arbitrary many of our own culture's "truths" really are.

The Cultural Connection

Sometimes called "bushmen" of the Kalahari, the !Kung San raise their children in a way that is consistent with other aspects of their lifestyle. For example, the San live communally and have little concept of privacy. As a result, babies are woven into the tribe's social fabric from birth. They are constantly surrounded by people; they are never left alone. And even though there is always someone back at camp who can baby-sit, infants go everywhere with their moms, who make their breasts available almost constantly. In San culture, it is clear that the relationship between mother and infant has special status.

Mobility is also very important to the !Kung San, who move from place to place depending on where they find food and water. Once again, the way children—particularly babies—are treated reflects this priority. For example, the San sling is designed to ensure that babies are held vertically. Infants who are left in a horizontal position won't develop proper motor skills, they believe. Babies are never put down on their backs as they are in the West. In fact, San parents, who let their children learn many things at their own pace, actually try to teach their little ones how to sit, stand and walk. Some of this training might just pay off: Research shows that San children appear to move better and earlier than their North American counterparts.

In Holland, parents hinge their attitudes on quite a different set of beliefs. The Dutch approach to baby care revolves around three Rs: *rust* (rest), *regelmaat* (regulation) and *rein held* (cleanliness). "Dutch parents bring to their child rearing an 'ethnohistory' or set of beliefs, which explains why infants need a great deal of sleep and must not be overstimulated neither during the day nor night," explains McKenna in his chapter "Cultural Influences on Infant and Childhood Sleep Biology and the Science that Studies It."

Sleep is only one area where different cultural values and beliefs are played out. A study conducted by child development researchers looked at the way three different cultures defined intelligence. Dutch parents said an intelligent child is strong-willed, persistent and clear in purpose, whereas Kipsigis African parents felt intelligence could be measured by the responsibility a child showed in doing her chores. American parents felt that an intelligent child is one who is aggressive and competitive.

In *Our Babies, Ourselves*, anthropologist Meredith Small points out that even what one culture considers "rules" of parenting are a mix of folk wisdom, tradition, fad and bits of science. Nowhere is this more dramatically evident than in the sphere of sleep.

"In almost all cultures around the globe today, babies sleep with an adult and children sleep with parents or other siblings. It is only in the industrialized Western societies such as North America and some countries in Europe that sleep has become a private affair," writes Small.

The African and Dutch examples are cases in point: A San baby would never be left alone to sleep, while Dutch babies almost always are. As for North America, Small explains that, "the chief overriding parental goal of American culture, whether stated overtly or not, is independence. In every study in which American parents were compared to other cultures, even other industrialized nations, American parents expressed over and over again the need to make a child independent and self-reliant." Small points out that this goal is a good match with many aspects of North American culture overall. After all, a big part of our social and economic structure is based on "getting ahead"—on individual achievement at work, on the private accumulation of material goods. Many of us want to "make a name for ourselves," to stand out in a crowd. And you have only to look at the way we worship celebrities to see the cult of the individual taken to the extreme.

All of this feeds the North American obsession with getting babies to sleep solo each and every night. Further, we tend to think of cribs as the "right" place for babies to bed down and, in fact, even believe them to be medically superior. But babies in other cultures sleep all kinds of other ways: in a hanging basket or a skin hammock, on a mat or blanket on the floor, on a mattress made of bamboo.

Is West Best?

Anthropologist Gilda Morelli, who studied Mayan Indians, their sleeping arrangements and their habits, found that Mayan babies slept with their mothers for the first year at least and sometimes the second as well, reports Small. (Dad was often there too, or he was sleeping with older children in another bed.) "Mayan mothers made no special note of feeding at night because they simply turned and made a breast available when the baby cried with hunger, probably while the mothers were still fast asleep," Small writes. This sharply contrasts the experience of many North American parents, who can't help but "note" nighttime feedings and the exhausting toll they take.

"The impression by many anthropologists," writes McKenna, "is that (in general) parents living in western industrialized societies are much less satisfied with how their children sleep than are parents in nonwestern societies, and that in industrialized societies nightly infant and childhood sleep comes about under more stressful conditions."

But that's not the only nighttime difference. Unlike North Americans, Mayan mothers didn't put their babies to bed with stories, snuggles or songs; there was none of the ritual so often associated with bedtime and so commonly endorsed by sleep experts. Rather, these Guatemalan mothers just went about their business and let their babies fall asleep—whenever.

While many North Americans might look askance at these practices or dismiss them as "ignorant," mothers from cultures whose child-rearing practices differ from our own aren't exactly falling over themselves to adopt the North American Way. When the researcher described to the Mayan moms how babies were put to bed in the U.S., they "were shocked and highly disapproving, and expressed pity for the American babies who had to sleep alone. They saw their own sleep arrangements as part of a larger commitment to their children, a commitment in which practical consideration plays no part," Small says.

Like the Mayan Indians, the Gusii of East Africa sleep with their babies. They also carry infants constantly, breastfeed them frequently and respond to their cries immediately. When Gusii mothers saw videotapes of their American counterparts, they were shocked at how long it took them to respond to their infants' cries.

"I was born and raised in Kenya and, though I myself spent time in a playpen and slept in a separate room and was wheeled around in a stroller, I remember from an early age seeing babies carried on their mums' backs, nursed on demand anywhere and everywhere, and taught responsibility through example and love. I am saddened by the 'distant' form of child rearing that appears to still be the norm in North America."
—Joanna Odrowaz

Naturally, each culture has its own daytime practices as well. While

North American parents are deeply concerned with development and stimulation, researchers found that Mayan mothers "did not see themselves as responsible for developing or shaping the baby's personality or mental abilities, but rather they were charged with keeping the baby quiet and comforted, away from harm," Small explains. To this end, mothers in the Yucatán kept their infants in hammocks in dark corners of their homes.

Similarly, North American mothers would probably see Gusii parents as unaffectionate. Says Small, "Mothers do not kiss and cuddle their babies and in fact appear comparatively aloof. Most striking to Western eyes is the fact that Gusii mothers do not interact verbally with their infants—they soothe and nurse, but consider conversation with infants a waste of time." Meanwhile, we coo at ours, play with them and bring them things to look at and touch.

Non-industrialized nations are not the only ones who approach kids' sleep differently. Half a world away, Japanese moms and dads also sleep with their babies.

Unlike North Americans, Japanese parents don't try to teach their babies independence or push separation. In fact, they feel that babies are born as separate entities who need to be drawn *into* an interdependent relationship with their parents—especially their mothers—and society. "For the Japanese, the concept of family includes sharing the night, and the model of the family tends to orient toward mother and children with the father on the outside, rather than the American version of the ideal nuclear family with mother and father as sacrosanct partners and children subordinate to that primary relationship," writes Small. Unlike America, the emphasis in Japan is on being part of a collective and finding one's place within society. Achieving individual success is less important than group harmony.

The Japanese are one of the most technologically and culturally sophisticated people in the world, and yet their approach to kids and sleep seems closer to that of the Mayan Indians or the Gusiis than to ours. This intrigued me so much that when Mari Takeda, a *Today's Parent* Sleep Survey respondent, invited me to join what she calls her "Japanese mothers' group" and do a little real-life research, I jumped at the chance.

The Japanese Way: Sleeping like a River

Mari gives me an address over the phone and a few days later, I am ringing a doorbell in a hip downtown Toronto neighborhood. As Chikaru Izumi, this week's hostess, welcomes me into her home, some preschoolers—one of them Chikaru's daughter, Kealani—peer at me curiously from the stairs. The sound of voices speaking staccato Japanese drifts out from the kitchen. At the table a toddler finishes his lunch, and a baby bounces happily on his mom's knee.

While I'm taking all this in, Chikaru is tossing around in her front hall closet. Then she looks at me and says, "Sorry, no more slippers." After a minute I realize this is her tactful way of asking me to take off my shoes.

I walk barefoot to the place they've left for me at the table and briefly introduce myself. Chikaru pours me a small glass of cold Japanese tea as she and the four other women, Mari, Ayako, Hiroko and Ikuko—all born and raised in Japan and living in Canada less than 10 years—begin to talk about their families and their night lives.

Plainspoken Mari goes first. "When Tyler [now 4] was a baby he didn't sleep at all. I'd feed him and try to put him to sleep and feed him and try to put him to sleep and feed him and try to put him to sleep—it could happen 13 times. It went on that way for two months. But then he suddenly started to sleep six-hour stretches. I was happy but the first few nights my breasts were rock hard!"

Tyler continued to sleep pretty well for a year and a half. But then, says Mari, "we went back to Japan for seven weeks and there we slept together. Tyler got so used to it that when we came back, he didn't like the crib anymore. So my husband went to a different room, and Tyler and I slept together in bed.

"After my second one, Luke, was born, I said forget about the crib, it's easier to have feeding and sleeping together. So Luke and I slept together in one bed, and my husband and Tyler in another."

But Mari is married to a Canadian man who isn't crazy about sleeping apart from his wife. "He says it's strange and nobody does it in Canada. He thinks sleeping with kids is the Japanese way," says Mari.

He's right on at least one count. I had read in Small that "Japanese babies and older children sleep between their parents to symbolize their position as a river between two banks, a being that is intimately connected to each parent as a river is to a riverbed." (Nancy Shand's *Culture's Influence in Japanese and American Maternal Role Perception and Confidence* is a more primary source for this information.) And, indeed, the women say that in Japan, families sleep "like the Chinese character of a river." It doesn't really make sense until Mari leans over my notebook and draws the symbol for "river":

"At first I thought it was a bit selfish," says Mari, getting back to her husband's preference for sleeping childless. "But then I began to realize that it *can* be hard to stay intimate when you don't have time to talk and be alone together. So now we have the boys [now 2 and 4] sleeping together, and we are together, and so far, it's successful."

Ayako Erenberg has boys as well, three of them: Aki, who is at school this afternoon, Mark, one of the preschool gang who thumps and giggles over our heads, and Max, the smiley baby who sits beside me at the table.

"With Aki," Ayako says, "we sat in the room with him and read the paper and waited for him to settle down and go to sleep. We were there but we kind of ignored him, and it worked."

"By the time we got to Max, we just needed to get some sleep, and we needed to be free for the other kids. So Max slept with us in our bed at first. Then we moved him to a crib where he now goes to sleep, but he wakes up around two and then we bring him into our bed."

Now Hiroko pipes up. "My first baby was born in Japan where we all slept together. By around three months, he was sleeping through the night." But things were quite different with baby number two. "He was born in Canada and he didn't sleep very well and I was lonely and depressed. He was almost 3 when he finally slept through the night." Hiroko doesn't assume that her first child slept better *because* he spent the night with his parents, but she does feel "the Japanese way" takes some of the stress out of having a baby. For example, in Japan it is very common for young mothers to pack themselves and their newborns up and go stay with their mothers for the first month or two postpartum, spending much of that time cocooned in bed together.

Chikaru and Ikuko have other stories to tell: 4-year-old Kealani slept between her parents for a few years but now sleeps in her own room. Sort of. "We lie down with her until she falls asleep. Then we sneak out of the room. She likes to fall asleep playing with my ear."

"Sorry. Your what?" I say, thinking I've misunderstood.

"My ear," nods Chikaru, and everyone chuckles.

Ikuko and her husband still sleep with their 1½-year-old, Izum. "Your husband doesn't mind?" asks Mari. "No, I think he likes it," says Ikuko, who suggested that her husband's heritage (he is Moroccan) may account for his flexible attitude toward kids and sleep. Still, Ikuko finds sleeping with Izum, who also nurses at night, tiring at times. "We tried sleep training, but it didn't work," she says. "He's a very light sleeper."

RIGHT UNDER OUR NOSES

You don't have to travel to the depths of the Kalahari Desert to find parents who approach sleep in unconventional ways. For one thing, we are a multicultural society so we have to expect—and respect—that the cultural backgrounds of North American parents will influence the way they think of and handle kids' sleep. Studies conducted in New York City, for example, found that both Hispanic- and African-Americans were more likely to sleep close to their babies than their white counterparts.

But ethnicity is not the only factor. Sleeping with babies and young children is the norm, for example, among a pocket of white Americans in eastern Kentucky (a.k.a. Appalachia) even though these parents are subject to the same independent-sleep dogma as the rest of us. This particular sub-culture simply rejects the notion that babies should sleep alone. Their goal, Meredith Small explains, "is to make a tightly knit family and keep children close." Verna Mae Sloane, an elderly Appalachian woman, puts it this way: "How can you expect to hold onto them in life if you begin by pushing them away?"

Sprinkled throughout North America, "attachment parents" are another group resistant to many of the ideas promoted by sleep specialists and other early-independence advocates. Coined by California pediatrician William Sears, the term "attachment parenting" refers to a style of child care that promotes closeness and contact—from responding quickly to a baby's cries, to using a baby carrier, to breastfeeding and bed-sharing. Says Sears, "Some people want babies to start being independent at a very early age. But for a child to be independent he has to go through a period of dependence first."

The individual stories are fascinating, but what can you conclude overall? What role does Japanese culture play in the sleep habits of these women and their families? At first I see no pattern. Each of these mothers has slept with a child at some point, but the group hasn't adopted co-sleeping universally, and some of the women don't particularly like it. A few have tried sleep training—successfully in one or two cases—but others never mention it.

And yet, there is something: Mari, Chikaru, Ayako, Hiroko and Ikuko are strikingly matter-of-fact about their sleep practices. When they talk about sleeping with their kids as a couple, or *letting* their husbands sleep alone (to get better rest) or *sending* them to sleep alone (to make more room), they are not coy or sheepish or apologetic. And when they talk about getting kids to sleep solo and processes like sleep training, they are not defensive or hypersensitive. The discussion takes place on an entirely practical level—what works, what doesn't—and never really moves into the heated realm it often does with North American parents. The reason is simple: Where kids sleep is not a big, emotionally charged issue in Japanese culture.

"In Japan you would be more embarrassed to tell someone you sleep with your husband than that you sleep with your kids," jokes Mari.

Lessons from the Global Village

Not everyone is intrigued by tales of parenting from around the world. Tracking these tidbits, I used to share them with a friend until she finally said, "So !Kung San mothers sleep with their kids and take them to work. They also live in huts and forage for their food. Does that mean we should, too?"

Of course it doesn't. Life in modern, industrialized society presents a set of living conditions vastly different from those imposed by tribal life, so many of our customs are not the same. Still, there isn't always a clear reason for doing things the way we do. We can study other cultures to loosen our focus on our own assumptions about parenting. It's easy to forget that there are more than one or two ways to diaper a baby, or promote motor skills or, yes, spend the night, until you take a step back and look around. That doesn't mean we should thoughtlessly adopt practices from other cultures or eras just for the sake of it. But if we can learn something about the essence of parenthood, about the rightness of our own instinct through the process, why not?

8 Beyond Weary

Y ou probably don't need to read a whole book to discover that the moms and dads of night wakers are a tired bunch. But the preceding chapters have shown that parents whose kids don't fit the 12-solid-hours'-sleep mold can end up with more than just a practical problem. We have seen how a variety of factors—the myths surrounding kids and sleep, the medicalized view of sleep "disorders," previous generations' attitudes, as well as a grab bag of contemporary cultural influences—have a profound effect on the way parents of wakeful kids feel. We have also learned that each baby is different from day one, so an individual child's temperament as well as her parents' own dispositions really matter, not just in terms of how much a child wakes at night, but also in terms of how that waking affects her parents' psyches. If all the parents we've talked to have shown us anything, it's that a complicated parcel of emotions accompany the seemingly pragmatic task of getting children to sleep at night.

The Unvarnished Truth

Parents of sleepless kids experience night waking in many ways—but keep reading, because not all of them are bad. But the truth is that negative emotions are the ones we tend to think of first.

Frustration, resentment, guilt...these feelings seem to be a big part of the night-waking package. For example, Joanna Slaight, mother of 18-month-old Carly, finds one of the most crazy-making aspects of night waking is the way it traps you in a catch-22. "You're exhausted and you would like to do whatever it takes to make the nights more peaceful for your family but you can't, because sleep training means you're going to get even less sleep before you get more, and you just *know* you will not survive that. I used to spend hours in the middle of the night trying to figure this out in my head, but I've stopped. I don't need to feel exasperated on top of exhausted." Simply put, you become too tired to solve the problem.

Guilt is a force to be reckoned with in far too many aspects of parenting, sleep prominent among them. Many sources throughout this book have talked about feeling guilty for letting their child cry at night or for "allowing" him to develop inferior sleep habits.

One survey respondent, Erika Van Straten, even went so far as to work out a theory: "I believe that the guilt associated with the early training attempts keep many parents from trying again at 12 or 18 months, when the child may actually be ready to sleep alone."

But it's a damned-if-you-do-damned-if-you-don't situation, since parents sometimes feel they will be judged negatively no matter how they handle night waking.

Anita has a perfectly legitimate take on kids' sleep; in fact, she does what most experts recommend, and what many parents feel they ought to do. And yet, she feels she has to justify it. "I know I don't share the most popular method or beliefs of babies and their sleep habits. I don't believe in family beds. I think it's important to keep the bedroom for my husband and myself. It's hard enough to continue a relationship in the bedroom without your children present. I feel I give my child plenty of love and affection during the days to know that she is not being neglected at night." When you consider that most family bedniks feel *they're* the ones who don't share the most popular beliefs about kids' sleep, you realize just how thorny an issue we're talking about.

A survey respondent named Angie spoke frankly about the feelings of resentment that are triggered by persistent night waking. "Christopher wakes up and wants drinks or a hug. I tend to get aggravated when this happens three or four times in one night. When it happens you just cannot function the next day.

"I find that sometimes when I wake up and have to go to him I am angry and I yell at him. But that just makes matters worse."

Many parents of night wakers are vulnerable to regret, as well. "I wish I had done a lot of things differently with my second child," says Kelly Vegso. "He was a difficult baby, and not particularly good in the night. His night waking lasted for nine months and I was exhausted for most of that time. I wish I had been more open to the idea of taking him into my bed. I don't know that that would've changed his sleep habits or behaviors, but it may have allowed me a few more precious hours of sleep. I found it difficult to be a good daytime parent to him because I was so exhausted."

But the news isn't all bad. For example, we heard from parents like Darlene Sherwood, who—believe it or not—find real joy in night waking. "Try to think about the time with your kids at night as quality

---

SLEEP SURVEY STATS
- 35% of *Today's Parent* Sleep Survey respondents "strongly agreed" with the statement: "It's important for parents to help their babies learn to fall asleep and stay asleep by themselves early in life."
- 67% of respondents "strongly agreed" with the statement: "It's important for parents to respond to their babies' cries, both day and night."

---

time (even though I hate that phrase). This is basic time between you and your child, without distractions of TV, phone or other people. Just enjoy and forget what other people think."

At first blush the idea of enjoying night waking seems pretty counterintuitive. Your eyes sting and your spine aches and you feel as if you've got lead blankets covering you when you try to get out of bed. You have to ignore the needs of every cell in your body so that you can take care of someone else's.

And yet, sometimes you do get nights when you feel as though you and your baby are an island of warmth and light in the cold, dark night. It's clear: His job is to need you and your job is to be needed. On a night like that, you can feel pretty sure that there's no better place to be than in that rocking chair (or futon or Lazy Boy) with that little someone who needs the sound of your breathing to fall asleep.

That Loving Feeling?

In the next chapter we will see how parents can work together—spelling each other off, offering moral support—to cope with night waking. But kids' sleep habits can also push parents apart.

As Holly Taylor says, "Having two parents can be a great positive and a disadvantage all at the same time. My spouse is extremely irritable in the wee hours of the night. He had a punctured ear drum when he was younger, so when the children cry—shriek—he flips out and heads for the furthest location from them. I'm left having to deal with the child who can't go to sleep and the irate husband who won't put ear plugs in his ears."

Alternatively, your partner might want to take an active role in nighttime parenting. But what if the two of you can't agree on how to handle it? Says one mom, "When I was ready to try techniques out, my husband wasn't. His technique was to carry her with her head on his shoulder. When he was exasperated and ready to try techniques, I wasn't. That was mainly because the tot would be fried by that time, so I would just take over by taking her into bed. He believed that carrying her was a way to bond with her. Who was I to interfere?"

The night-waking experience can be so harrowing that some parents consider closing up shop. Says Jo-Anne Weston, "I have three boys. My first son (now 14) slept through the night at about six months. My second son, born 19 months later, did not sleep through the night until he was 4½ years old. My spouse did not want to have any more children because of the second child's sleep behavior. It took me six years to talk him into having another one."

All this before you even begin to consider how wakeful children affect the intimate side of your relationship. Just look at my friends Sarah and Kevin, who asked me not to use their real names.

By 8:30 on most nights, Sarah has already washed her face, brushed her teeth and changed into one of the big T-shirts she likes to sleep in. She usually gets 6-month-old Daniel down around 8 p.m. and doesn't like to waste any time getting into bed herself. Invariably she's exhausted and knows the night ahead is unlikely to be more restful than the one just past.

Meanwhile, Kevin, her husband, puts in long hours at work. He gives Daniel his bath whenever he can, but more often, Sarah and Daniel go through the bedtime routine as a twosome. On these nights, Kevin arrives home after dark, quickly rummages around in the fridge if he hasn't had dinner, then hurries up the stairs. But when he finds Sarah, she is often snoring softly. "Not again," he groans as he heads back downstairs to check the mail and watch TV.

Days can go by before Sarah and Kevin get the opportunity to have a face-to-face heart-to-heart, let alone something more. Anyone who does a lot of nighttime duty (and not all are women) can probably relate to Sarah's priorities. Some of their partners may very well identify with Kevin's frustration.

John Hoffman, a father of three and a night-waking veteran, understands both. "When your baby wakes up a lot, it's just really hard—you're tired, and sleep becomes this crucialized commodity. The hierarchy of needs changes. When you're in the night-waking head space all you can think about is getting sleep and that's not conducive to sex."

"My wife did most of the night stuff," explains Hoffman. "She had better tolerance. She could get out of bed, do what she had to do and go back to sleep within 10 minutes. If I did it I would be up for ages. I did the morning stuff. When Riley [now 15] was a baby, there were times when I would get up at 5:30 and then put him down for his first nap before Holly was even up."

Since Hoffman (a musician and a writer) has spent time in the driver's seat as a primary caregiver, he also sees how stay-at-home parenting can dampen desire. "When you're holding babies most of the day, your physical craving for touch is less."

However in tune, Hoffman didn't stop being human just because there was a restless baby in the house. "All these things didn't affect my desire as much as they did hers," he says. "I still wanted sex. I wanted more sex than there was. I sometimes got mad about it."

So what did he do? "I learned that it worked better for her if she could say, 'It's going to be tomorrow,'" says Hoffman. "Then I could do something to make sure she got rest that day, or to make sure she got time to herself. She used to say to me, 'You've got to get to me before my head hits the pillow.'"

By their third child, John and Holly had figured out how to make sure that night waking and lovemaking weren't mutually exclusive.

"We adopted a pattern that would probably make a marriage counsellor's hair stand on end," says Holly. "John slept on the spare mattress in the attic. I slept in our queen with Aaron [the baby]. I slept undisturbed, because I had all this room. It was easy to look after Aaron in the night. John got a decent rest, or read into the wee hours if he had to without waking me up. And he got up early in the morning with the kids, and I slept most days till 8 or 8:30. It worked great.

"And you know, it didn't wreck our sex life," says Holly. "I would say our post-baby sex was *better* after Aaron than the other two, because I wasn't so tired, and because we had this little hideaway in the attic that felt a bit like a crummy hotel that was kind of fun."

Finding a way to hang on to some intimacy in your relationship with your partner isn't easy when you have little kids; it can be even tougher when those little kids don't sleep through the night. But as John, Holly and my friends who keep pillows and a blanket stashed in their bathroom closet know, a little bit of creativity can make a big difference. The trick is to let go of your assumptions about what is "ideal" or "right" and look, instead, for what works.

9 Whatever Gets You Through the Night

Once you let go of the notion that there is a single right way to get babies and children to sleep at night, a funny thing happens: You start to find sleep strategies everywhere. And since it's clear that experts can't always know what's best for individual parents, anyone's solution is a viable option.

The little piece of wisdom that eases your sleep crunch may come from the parent next door, a respondent to the sleep survey or the 10-year-old who heard I was writing this book and called to relay a strategy that "worked every time with my little sister." It is in this spirit that I present the following grab bag of tips, tales and anecdotes. I pass them on without judgment or analysis; they are not "recommended," but they have been field-tested by other parents. They are broadly grouped according to the two problems they address: how to get a child to sleep better, and how parents can cope when they're not getting enough rest.

GETTING SOME SHUT-EYE, PART 1:
Bring Baby Close

The ideas collected in this section are alike in that they involve getting close to your baby in order to promote sleep—hers and yours.

The Family Bed
Says Karyn Kirkwood, "I told my husband we were pregnant by saying, 'It's time to buy the king-sized bed.' We knew we would do the family bed, although I knew no one who did. And so we bought a king-sized bed. It was the best purchase we ever made.

"By co-sleeping, my daughter and I did achieve that synchronicity described by William and Martha Sears in *The Baby Book*. I would often wake just before her and sometimes would even have a let-down before she woke so that my milk would be ready for her.

"I was never able to sleep through nursing the way some family-bed advocates describe. However, by sharing sleep, I was never abruptly ripped out of a deep sleep and I would often doze during a nursing. And when my daughter had her fill, she would roll over to sleep and I would quickly follow her to dreamland.

"Despite some people's concerns that she'll be sleeping with us when she's 18, I know that someday she will outgrow her need for nighttime comfort just like she's outgrown her need for diapers and naps. Besides, I haven't met an 18-year-old yet who would want to share a bed with her parents!"

John Mac Phee says, "My wife is Chinese from Taiwan. She grew up in a family bed situation mostly due to economic circumstances and had nothing but good things to say about it. I on the other hand, was raised in a crib from the day I was born and was bottle fed. When my son was born we had a crib all set up for him but after trying just a couple of times at letting him sleep in it in the afternoon my wife decided to nurse him to sleep in our bed as she and I didn't think that it was right to torment the poor little guy by making him cry himself to sleep. It is now 7 years later and I think that we made the right decision in using the family bed method. Our son is well adjusted, not overly dependent."

But Do They Ever Leave?

This is a burning question in the minds and hearts of many parents who have brought their children into bed, or have considered it. For some parents, reclaiming their bed is a snap; others find it takes a little more finagling...and a little more time.

Amanda Knox falls into the first group. "By the time Aerik was 3 months old we all moved into our bed. Our little boy slept in our bed until he was 9 months old and walking. We then placed his crib mattress on the floor in the corner of our room and made a little bed for him.

And there he slept, content to be near his parents and not to be in a crib. After five months, we purchased a full-sized, child bed. It was complete with a Winnie the Pooh sheet and comforter set—and set up in his own room. Aerik has slept in his own bed most nights since then."

Jocelyn Chan used a similar strategy. "My two boys, age two and four, slept through the night just after the first month. I guess we're considered one of the lucky few—although I do strongly believe that this wouldn't be so without the practice of the family bed. My boys shared our bed until they were one year and then we gradually weaned them off by having them sleep in a crib in our room, then moving the crib into their own room while we slept beside them on a futon. Within a month they were sleeping in their own room without us. Of course, we also gave them the opportunity to decorate their rooms and make them their own."

Here's how Nancy Mugford managed the transition: "My children both slept in a family bed, the first till 2½ and the second till 3. I nursed them back to sleep until then. After that I lay beside them [in their beds] to get them used to sleeping in their own beds. After a few weeks, I insisted they come to me at night. When they had to get up and come to our bed the frequency of night waking diminished."

The reclaiming process took a little longer in Barb Botelho's household: "We allowed our child to sleep with us until about 4 years of age and then began training him to stay in his own bed for the night. We used a sticker chart to encourage this."

Share My Sleep but Not My Bed

I used to think of "co-sleeping" and bed sharing as pretty much the same thing. Now I realize many parents sleep close to their kids without sharing a bed.

"[From birth,] Arerik refused to let me put him down for very long, and cried whenever we would place him in his bassinet," recounts Amanda Knox. "Being a neo-mother and therefore very new to the breastfeeding experience, I had a difficult time feeding him while lying in bed. I also found it extremely difficult to get up and nurse him in a chair several times a night—he was nursing every 45 minutes at one point. Eventually, I opted to sleep in a recliner chair in the living room with Aerik nestled happily on my chest. When he got hungry I would move him into the nursing position, change sides, burp him and we would drift off to sleep again. My husband chose to sleep on the couch so that he would be nearby."

For the Talalla family, the fit is in the futon: "[Two-year-old] Ethan goes to sleep in his own bed—a single futon on the floor surrounded by pillows—in his own room," says Ethan's mom, Dana. "When my husband is working late, Lucas [3 months] and I lie down beside him. We read books and sing a couple of songs. Then Ethan rubs my elbow or knuckle until he falls asleep.

"When he wakes in the night—anywhere between 1 a.m. and 5 a.m.—he calls for us, and one of us arrives and joins him on the futon. Then he gives his instruction: 'Mommy lie down. Ethan head on Mommy.' If I'm in the middle of feeding Lucas and Ethan wakes up, then I take Lucas with me. Sometimes we wake up together like that."

"[My daughter] sleeps on a mattress beside our bed so there is never any 'getting up' to go see her, or any feeling of desertion on her part," says Daniele Bajus. "She can look up in the morning and see mommy lying up there. If she needs to come up, she is able to climb up. This is a real help now that I am pregnant and too tired some nights to get up. If she weren't right there, I'd be wearing myself out."

Compromises

Maybe you want to go to bed as a couple, but you don't mind waking up in the morning as a threesome (or foursome?). That's where Nancy Lawrance can help you: "While both my children usually end up in bed with us at some point in the night, my 9-month-old starts out in her crib most nights because she has an earlier bedtime than we do. Safety is important so if we are not settled in bed for the night, we do not allow her to sleep on the bed unattended."

For other parents, bringing the baby's crib into the master bedroom is the best solution. "My son has always slept for two to three hours and then wakes up for feedings. I have tried from the fourth month to space this out longer but after a month of trying to train him, I realized that

---

SLEEP SURVEY STATS

We asked: "After 4 months of age, what did you usually do when your child woke up at night?"

Here's how parents answered (Note that respondents could choose more than one answer, so the total percentage adds up to more than 100):

84% nurse/give a bottle

78% give physical comfort (rocking, cuddling, singing)

56% bring baby into bed

47% give a soother

31% use a sleep training method

---

he needed the feedings and established a routine that would make it easier for me to get some sleep," says Mylene Collet. "I now have the crib at the foot of my bed and when he wakes in the night, I have a bottle of milk handy to give to him from my bed. Once he is finished, the bottle goes back to the spot on the floor and back to sleep we go. Since I implemented this method, he only wakes twice during the night instead of every two to three hours so I get a few more hours of sleep."

Jacqueline Waechter found an unusual way to support her daughter's sleep. "When we'd put her to bed, we would sleep on the floor beside her, but not touch her or take her out of the crib. So if she cried, we would say, 'It's OK, we're here.' We stayed in the room as long as we needed to. This lasted less than a month, and then she was sleeping through till morning."

GETTING SOME SHUT-EYE, PART 2:
Helping Baby Go Solo

If you are one of the many parents who prefer sleep solutions that teach babies to sleep on their own, you're in luck—we've amassed an interesting collection.

Most expert advice falls squarely in this area. Richard Ferber's method, which involves leaving your child for short but increasing intervals until he falls asleep, is likely the most well-known and has worked for many parents. Here is Karen Whalen Billard's own Ferber interpretation: "I always check [my daughter] every five minutes when she cries and kiss the top of her head and tell her I love her, but don't pick her up—she usually settles in 4 to 12 minutes. I watch the clock as it seems like it goes on forever and I need the reassurance that it hasn't been hours."

"We found a book we liked," says Sonja Whitchurch, *"Helping Your Child Sleep Through the Night* by Joanne Cuthbertson and Susanna Schevill." Sonja and her husband tried the authors' method for gradually decreasing night feedings: "Nursing for four minutes on each side for two nights, and then three minutes etc." If the baby is still waking after you've gone down to one minute, the authors recommend introducing a bottle, "half water and half breast milk or formula and then just water." Unfortunately, says Whitchurch, "Molly hadn't read the book and it was not successful"—but it might be for you.

A friend who asked me not to use her name felt she *had* to get her 10-month-old sleeping through the night but found that the Ferber method and all those check-ins were too stimulating for her little boy. So she took Weissbluth's advice and went cold turkey. "It was one week of hell, and then it was over. We haven't had much trouble since."

Put Him Down Awake

"My mother gave me the best piece of advice concerning sleep training," says Catherine Laxton-Godberson. "I have had five boys and I had no trouble with any of them. The advice was to always put your newborn down awake. My babies always lay awake a few minutes looking around the crib. Before I knew it they were asleep, and I continued this pattern and they learned to go to sleep on their own. At first it is difficult, because your urge is to cuddle them until they fall blissfully asleep in your arms. It is a warm and lovely maternal feeling. However, you pay for it in spades when the baby will not go down without being held and cuddled."

Loree Burnham describes a similar approach in greater detail: "I would have my young baby's cradle in the kitchen or living room during the day. This way they would nap in a fairly bright and often noise-filled room.

"At night, the cradle would be moved back into either my room (if the baby was only a few months old) or their room. I would have the room rather dark except for the night-light. Just enough light to allow me to see them, change them, nurse them. When my babies were very young, I would try to nurse them long enough to fill their bellies. By changing their bums between breasts, it would rouse them enough to nurse the second side. At 4 months or so, they are quite good at getting a lot of milk fast, so I didn't worry so much about keeping them awake longer.

"I would try to put my babies down for a sleep while they were still awake, but ready for sleep, hence their being able to put themselves back to sleep whenever they would wake up during the night without my ever knowing they were awake."

Routines, Rituals and Schedules

When he was first walking and becoming really active, my younger son, Leo, went through a phase where he would wake in the middle of the night and want to go downstairs to play. This was a terrific problem. It would be 4 a.m. and we couldn't see straight but he'd cry and point and lean and flail until we took him out of bed and headed for the stairs.

The solution came in the form of a bedtime ritual: Before bed, we went around the entire house saying good night to everything—"Good night TV, good night red car, good night kitchen, good night good food, good night blue fish..." on and on we'd go. And then I'd say, "All of the toys and foods and furniture we use during the day are going to sleep now, just like you. We won't see them again until it's light outside." I can't say this was the end of Leo's career as a night waker, but it did nip that particular habit in the bud.

For Kelly Arns, scheduling was the key. "The biggest change from my first to second child was that I kept a rigid schedule for number two. I knew that I didn't want the same problems we experienced with our firstborn. Bedtime at approximately the same time nightly with the same routine (nursing, story, rocking, then crib). That, along with a regular daily routine (for naps, snacks and meals), really made the difference."

Michelle Torraville relates, "My husband and I take turns giving our son his night bottle before he goes to bed. This is done in his room with soft music playing and him being rocked. During the day when he goes down for a nap, I turn on his music, pull his blinds down, hug him and kiss him and let him fall asleep on his own, because I am unable to rock him during the day due to working. He is 10½ months old and he is getting used to this more and more. He will cry sometimes for maybe five minutes but if it is any longer then I go back in to calm him down again. On the whole, he does fall asleep by himself during the day."

Parents Get Creative

Even if these ideas don't work for you, they're bound to trigger some innovations of your own.

"To ensure that our son, Joshua, could find a pacifier if he woke up," says Cheryl Yaffa, "we placed half a dozen pacifiers in the crib near him. He quickly learned how to reach out and pop one into his mouth then fall back asleep."

Flora Morton learned this pearl of wisdom from her sister for winter babies who jump awake when you transfer them from your warm, cuddly breast or bed to their cold, empty cribs: "When the baby wakes up, fill up a hot water bottle and slip it under the crib blanket. When he falls asleep, you sidle up to the crib, remove the hot water bottle (one-handed, of course), pull back the warm covers, and lay the baby down in the warm spot. (Maybe first make sure it's not *hot*.) Keep your hand on him until he seems to have settled in (an attempt to trick him into thinking you're still right there beside him). Then cover him up with your deluxe prewarmed covers."

Here's what helped Gail Abell's little girl: "When it was dark we said good night to her toys and stuffed animals and laid them at the end of her bed and they would go to sleep."

"I'd give him a cloth diaper to suck on," says one mom. "I don't know why this works, but he liked to have a piece of cloth in his mouth to go to sleep!"

"We got our child attached to a blankie for comforting," says Susanne Mohsenian simply.

Laurie Edwards's routine is a bit more involved. "Now that my daughter is almost three, *Goodnight Moon* is one of her favorite stories," she explains. When Jessica awakens, "Instead of saying 'In the great green room, there was a telephone and a red balloon,' I say, 'In Jessica's pink room, there is no telephone, but the light of the moon, to help us see the picture of the mermaid, and the little bunnies sitting on the shelf, and the Barbie house that is fit for a mouse...' and then I let her name the items in the room, and it works wonderfully."

"If all else failed," wrote Renee on a *Today's Parent* Online forum, "then I would close my eyes and pretend to have fallen asleep. [My daughter] seemed to feel comforted by that because within five minutes she was always out."

Does That Really Work?

If you're tired enough, you will try almost anything. And—surprise, surprise—sometimes those way-out ideas actually get results.

"The best thing we did was on the recommendation of a pediatrician," says Melissa McCowan. "She met our son, a year old, [and] said, 'He's a bright boy. Explain what you need from him.' That night, I told him that we both needed more sleep, and to please try to go back to sleep alone, but I'd be there if he needed me. He slept for six hours, falling asleep on his own twice (at least.) They're smarter than we give them credit for being."

"Since the beginning," says Trish Snyder, "Rylie had been having trouble with sleep—or *I* had been having trouble with his sleep. It was getting really frustrating for me and I was willing to try anything. My mother-in-law sells pads that are filled with magnetic fibers and are supposed to balance the body's energies. She believed that if Rylie slept on this pad, it would help his body fall into deeper sleep. We put it in the crib and that night he slept for seven hours straight and I thought, 'Oh my god, eureka!' He was 2½ months at the time and he had only done this once before. A week went by before he had another long sleep.... Then he got a cold, and we didn't want to leave him. But for the last week or so, we've been using the pad and he seems to have started sleeping better. It could be a coincidence but at the same time, I'm not taking it out of his crib!"

"The best thing I was ever given," Rose Berezowsky reveals, "was a baby soother tape. You need to start using the tape before 6 weeks of age. I started at 4 weeks, and it worked wonders. The children fell asleep themselves. I continued to use the tape until they were about a year and we have never had problems with them falling asleep."

AFTER A ROUGH NIGHT

In addition to asking parents to share their best sleep strategies, our survey invited parents of night wakers to explain how they cope the day after. By far the most frequently mentioned methods were the two most obvious:

Taking naps

"I napped when she did. Ate a good breakfast, took vitamins," writes Sherry Wallace. "We all had a long afternoon nap together in my bed. I found the kids napped better with me than without me," says Kim Martignago.

Enjoying lots of java

Audrey Vermeer pretty well sums up that strategy by saying, "I have an extra cup of coffee and enjoy the day with my children like I would any day!"

Karen Yahara goes for a different type of stimulant. "I take a nap if possible. If not, try to get some **exercise** to get the blood pumping."

Change Your Attitude

Although it's not always easy, parents are sometimes able to overcome exhaustion just by putting it in perspective.

We've all been there: you finally get the baby back to sleep, and *you* become the one with the night-waking problem. Whether it's from worry about how tired you're going to be tomorrow or when you're going to have to wake up next, it's easy to develop insomnia when you've got a night waker.

Here's what Teresa Pitman did: "My mother told me that even if you can't sleep, if you relax your body as much as possible it's almost as good. So I would go through one of those conscious relaxation exercises (tighten the muscle, then relax it) and relax my body as much as possible so that I was getting rest, if not sleep.

"I also found it very helpful psychologically to turn the clock around so I couldn't see it. It makes night waking so much worse if you're lying there looking at the clock and thinking 'Oh no, it's 5 a.m. and I have to get up in two hours.' I would also deliberately not count how many times the baby woke during the night. Those things really helped me to go with the flow."

"I cope on days when I am tired by thinking of our next-door neighbor (the mom) who has five children," writes Holly Albersworth. "At midnight, five days a week she leaves for work in a chip factory and returns at 8:30 a.m., when her husband leaves for work. She is lucky on days when her husband can work at home. She does this because she finds it hard for her family to exist on one income. If I feel tired, I can just think about Patsy and realize what tired really is."

M. Wellman says, "I just grin and bear it. You can choose to be tired and happy or tired and grumpy. It's really up to you."

Don't Push It
Several moms found the best way to get through the day after a sleepless night is to take it easy.

"I try to get rest whenever I can and try not to set expectations for myself in regards to getting housework done," says one.

"I find not doing a single thing but playing with my daughter helps restore energy and reinforce the sense that it was and will always be worth the sleepless nights," says another.

"If possible," says Krista Davy, "we have a quiet day with movies, playdough and board games that can be played on the floor."

"We both usually end up sleeping in late," says Barb Botelho.

If You Work Outside Your Home...
Sleeping in and playing your child's favorite videos won't be possible.

Here are some other ideas: "When I went back to work, I napped at lunchtime (so much for fancy executive lunches) and went to bed earlier at night," says D. Smith.

"I have a supervisor who is a very good, understanding mother of two. Sometimes we share work more than usual," writes another mom who works outside her home.

"I call my friends or my partner for help, take a good shower before going to work and a nap after work," explains Diane Gallant.

Here's a simple little trick of my own: I try not to talk about how tired I am or how little sleep I've had. I've found that this works much better than walking around the office complaining and looking for sympathy, because, well, the most sympathetic listener was always me! It's like reminding yourself to feel bad.

Lean on Me

Sometimes I tell myself that if I were a really competent mom, I would be able to manage without help. Of course, this is ridiculous. It is both smart and practical to get help when you need it.

When two parents are on duty, good teamwork can make the difference between sinking and swimming. Angela Taylor says, "How could it be possible that this beautiful, precious bundle of joy needs only 20 minutes sleep at a time, no matter whether it is day or night? I know I asked myself that very question with both my boys. I can remember sitting in my rocking chair and nursing my oldest for five hours straight one night and ending up in tears about the fact that he just would not sleep. We tried soothers. We tried car rides, which only worked for as long as the car was moving. We tried everything and anything anyone suggested to us. I love my boys and I sure wouldn't give them up for the world, but the ultimate answer for me was to give them to their Daddy and crawl right back into bed. Night night."

Terri Orlando also found the key to dealing with night waking was a solid partnership: "On the nights when I get frustrated, I cry with my daughter or I go and get my darling husband and he walks her to sleep and will even fall asleep in the lounge chair in the bedroom with her. On weekends, my husband will take the baby and I go back to bed for a couple of hours. That also gives me something to look forward to."

Or maybe it's someone other than your partner who picks up the slack. "I just started by having her grandfather near her when she sleeps. He pats her back if she wakes and speaks softly to her. It's only been one week, and she appears to be waking a little less every night," says Holly Albersworth.

Even if they can't do night duty for you, extended family or other helpers can make a difference. "My mother was always fabulous about coming over on a moment's notice to take the kids to the park or the mall so that I could crawl into bed—just as I was ready to crack," recalls Barbara Wells.

"By the time I got to four children, I hired a babysitter to come for an hour or two after school and before supper—the hardest part of the day for me. It is perfectly legitimate to hire a babysitter so that you can take a nap! And I did," says Teresa Pitman.

So there you have it—a meaty but by no means exhaustive list of strategies to try out the next time Mr. Sandman skips your house. You don't have to stop here, though. Ask around. Poll your neighbors, relatives, friends and colleagues. Once you drag your nightlife into the daylight, others will do the same. You will always find something you can use.

10 Happy Endings

T his book offers no guaranteed cure for kids' wakefulness except maybe this one: time. Every parent of every child who needs help falling asleep at night or in the night should know that this stage doesn't last forever. Simply keeping that in mind won't always be enough to get you through the night. But if you tuck this little tidbit into a drawer in your mind, you can pull it out on really tough days and try it on like a treasured-but-still-too-tight sweater. And, surprise, surprise, one day you'll find that it fits. "The night they did sleep through came just as I was ready for the looney bin," remembers Angela Taylor, "and I really didn't even notice it until the next morning."

For some families, the problem does literally disappear overnight.

For others it kind of peters out.

Penny Qualls says, "I have sat or laid down with each of my children at different ages to help them fall asleep. A lot of people shun me for this. They say that my kids will need help getting to sleep till they are much older. That they will have sleeping problems when they are grown. I don't believe it for a minute. My 11-year-old goes to bed when it's his bedtime, no fuss. The 6-year-old is beginning to fall asleep by herself after a story and sometimes a back rub or back scratch. Our youngest is giving us the most trouble about sleeping—he likes to go to sleep in our bed. It does make for some tired mornings, but we know from the other two kids that this won't last forever."

And it doesn't, says Heather Brill. "After spending the better part of a decade doing night duty followed by dawn patrol with three kids (none of whom slept through the night until around age 3), I can report that it does get better. Holidaying at a cottage last year, my husband and I found ourselves not only sleeping all night, but enjoying long, quiet mornings to ourselves while the kids—now 6, 10, and 13—slept late. It was amazing. Sometimes they slept so long I got bored and woke them up. Sometimes they complained that my husband's (or my own?) snoring woke *them* in the night!"

In still other families, the children simply become old enough (or competent enough) to manage their own needs without rousing their parents. "I think he's up most nights," says Gail Becker of 4-year-old Thomas. "But I'm not really sure. I'll hear the toilet flush or his door creak. Once in a while I'll even hear him talking to himself, something he does for comfort. But it's rare that he actually wakes us in the night."

Whether it burns out or fades away, night waking can leave some unexpected emotions behind. "I, for one," says Jenn Nicholls, "miss rocking and crooning and stroking my daughter's cheek or hair while I soothe her to sleep. Now it's hard just to get a 10-second cuddle out of her. (She is 5.) The point: Kids grow up and they grow up fast. Soon they won't need us at all. Parents should take this time to feel the importance of the incredible impact we make in their young lives. OK, OK, ask me the same question when I've been sleep deprived."

Like birth, you forget just how painful this aspect of parenthood can be almost as soon as it's over. Right up front, Kim Martignago says, "Night waking is not a problem in our house and I'm not currently sleep deprived so it's easy for me to have this opinion." Still, "I think that kids need to know you're there for them even in the middle of the night. You just do whatever you need to. If that means they sleep in your bed or on the floor beside your bed or you in their bed with them, so be it. I have yet to hear of a 14-year-old wanting to crawl into bed with his or her parents. Just remember: When they're teenagers, we'll be complaining that all they do is sleep!"

Being a parent is about holding on tight and letting go. Sometimes you're just getting used to doing one when it's time to switch to the other. I can't say that I really *enjoy* getting up with my kids at night—if I had the choice, I think I'd skip the whole night-waking thing in a heartbeat. And yet, when my now-9-year-old stopped waking up at 3 or 4 a.m. to croak, "Juice please, Mommy," I really was sad. I felt a similar melancholy when I dropped him off for his first day of preschool and when he learned to ride a two-wheeler. I even felt it last summer when I put him on the bus for his first-ever session of sleepover camp. Being needed so intensely and passionately is hard, but being needed not so passionately is hard, too.

There is nothing quite like the total body-and-soul marathon you run while your kids are little. Love it or loathe it, you've got to remember that it's fleeting. "My 6-year-old wet the bed the other night—a very rare occurrence now, but fairly common in earlier years," says Jane Cook. "We went right into our old routine—he put on dry pajamas and climbed into our bed to warm up while I changed his sheets. When I came back to get him, he was cuddled right up to his dad, fast asleep. I was kind of stricken looking at them, realizing we might never do this again, remembering how many of the endearing, tender moments with our kids had occurred in the middle of the night. No, I won't miss stumbling around stripping off wet sheets, but I can get a lump in my throat thinking about that cold little boy drifting happily off to sleep between us."

Mantra for Nighttime Parents

The purpose of this page: To help you avoid wasting precious energy beating yourself up about night waking. Take this list—a condensed version of some ideas presented throughout the book—and put it on your bedside table; cut it out and pin it to your baby's bedroom door; stick it to your fridge. Whatever you do, let it make you feel better. That's what it's for.

- I'm a good parent.

- My child's night waking is not my fault.

- My child's night waking may be a practical problem, but it's not a psychological or a moral problem.

- There is nothing wrong with my child.

- Babies who sleep more aren't "better."

- I am not the only one. Lots of really great kids with good parents don't sleep through the night.

- Sleep needs are affected by temperament, and babies have varying sleep needs from birth.

- Sleep training doesn't work for every child.

- There is nothing wrong with bringing my child into bed with me or comforting him back to sleep, if that's what works for us.

- There is nothing wrong with letting my baby cry a little at night, if that's what works for us.

- Night waking doesn't last forever.

Appendix
THE *TODAY'S PARENT* SLEEP SURVEY RESULTS

Methodology: The *Today's Parent* Sleep Survey was posted on the *Today's Parent* website from July 9 to August 27, 1999. A total of 1,484 responses were collected. In the August edition of *Today's Parent* magazine, an invitation to participate in the survey was posted on the Editor's page. An additional 72 surveys were mailed out to parents who called in to request the survey and were used for reading purposes only. Two hundred and thirty-seven respondents e-mailed in additional comments regarding their sleep experiences.

Because very young babies have not established much "sleep history," only parents who had at least one child 9 months or older were invited to complete the survey.

---

1. How many children do you have in the following age groups? (%)

	1	2	3+		1	2	3+
0 to 6 months	13	.4	.2	7 to 12 months	20	.3	.3
1 and 2 years	53	2	.3	3 to 5 years	35	5	.6
6 to 8 years	17	2	2	9 to 12 years	7	2	.3

2. You are: 7% a single parent 93% living with a partner

3. Your age:

.1%	under 18	10%	18 to 24
68%	25 to 34	19%	35 to 49
3%	40 to 44	.5%	45+

When answering the rest of the questionnaire, please consider your experience with your youngest child who is *9 months or older.*

4. Did you, or are you currently, breastfeed(ing)?

        75% yes   25% no

5. If yes, approximately how long did you/do you plan to breastfeed?

17%	less than 4 months	25%	4 to 7 months
28%	8 to 12 months	15%	13 to 18 months
7%	19 to 24 months	8%	more than 24 months

6. If we defined "sleeping through the night" as sleeping most nights from your child's bedtime until he/she wakes up for the day, does your child sleep through the night?

        70% yes   30% no

7. If yes, at what age did he/she begin to consistently sleep through the night?

29%	less than 4 months	27%	4 to 7 months
20%	8 to 12 months	10%	13 to 18 months
6%	19 to 24 months	8%	more than 24 months

8. After 4 months of age, what did you usually do when your child woke up at night? (Note: % will not add up to 100. Respondents could choose more than one answer.)

84% nurse/give a bottle

56% bring to bed

47% give a soother

78% give physical comfort, rock, cuddle, sing, etc.

31% use a sleep training method

If you did not use a training method, please go to question 14.

9. Describe the technique you tried most often when training your child to sleep through the night.

_____

_____

10. How old was your child when you started to train him/her to sleep through the night?

20%   less than 4 months   36%   4 to 7 months

31%   8 to 12 months   9%   13 to 18 months

3%   19 to 24 months   2%   more than 24 months

11. Overall how would you rate the success of the technique you tried?

52% very successful   25% partially successful

12% somewhat unsuccessful   11% very unsuccessful

12. Overall how did you feel about the training process?

34% very comfortable   28% somewhat comfortable

27% somewhat stressed   11% very stressed

13. Would you use this technique on another baby?

68% yes   9% no   24% not sure

Please explain:

14. If you did not use a sleep training method, please explain why not.

15. To what extent do you agree or disagree with the following statements:

	Agree Strongly	Agree Somewhat	Disagree Somewhat	Disagree Strongly
It's important for parents to help their babies learn to fall asleep and stay asleep by themselves early in life.	35%	42%	13%	10%
It's important for parents to respond to their babies' cries, both day and night.	67%	29%	4%	.3%

Night waking has been a big problem in our family.	12%	22%	26%	40%
Night waking after a few months of age is not normal.	4%	17%	33%	47%
Babies sleep through the night at different ages because of differences in how parents handle bedtime and night waking.	20%	44%	23%	14%
Babies sleep through the night at different ages because of differences in temperament and individual development.	57%	39%	3%	.8%

16. Do you think there is an ideal place for young babies to sleep at night?

        70% yes   30% no

17. If yes, where?

        43% in a crib, in their own room

        16% in a crib, in their parents' room

        11% in their parents' bed

18. Has your child ever slept in bed with you?

14% yes, every night   27% yes, often

42% yes, occasionally   17% no

19. How did you/do you cope after a night of being up a lot with your child?

_____

_____

_____

20. Which of the following experts' approaches to sleep have you read/heard of?

21. Which approach(es) do you agree with?

	Heard of/ read about	Agree with
Richard Ferber	74%	25%
William Sears	51%	28%
Penelope Leach	49%	21%
T. Berry Brazelton	36%	7%

22. Did your expectations of, and approach to, your baby's night waking change from your oldest child to your youngest child?

Change in Expectations   74% no   26% yes   How?

_____

_____

_____

Change in Approach   76% no   24% yes   How?

_____

_____

_____

23. Where, would you say, do your attitudes about children and sleep originate from? (check all that apply)

95% my partner's beliefs   89% my baby's behaviour

72% what I have read   49% friends and peers

44% my own instincts   43% my parents or other
relatives

Index